Information and joining up services

The case of an information guide for parents of disabled children

Bridgette Wessels and Val Bagnall

The POLICY PRESS

First published in Great Britain in September 2002 by

The Policy Press
34 Tyndall's Park Road
Bristol BS8 1PY
UK

Tel   +44 (0)117 954 6800
Fax   +44 (0)117 973 7308
e-mail tpp@bristol.ac.uk
www.policypress.org.uk

British Library Cataloguing in Publication Data

A catalogue record for this book is available from the British Library

ISBN 1 86134 429 5

Bridgette Wessels is Lecturer in the Department of Sociological Studies, University of Sheffield and was formerly Senior Research Associate, University of Newcastle upon Tyne; **Val Bagnall** was Interagency Development Worker (Children with Disabilities), Health and Social Services, Newcastle upon Tyne until October 2001.

Cover design by Qube Design Associates, Bristol.

Front cover: Photograph kindly supplied by www.third-avenue.co.uk.

Printed and bound in Great Britain by Henry Ling Ltd, Dorchester.

Contents

Acknowledgements

The former Joint Consultative Committee in Newcastle upon Tyne funded the two-year interagency post of Development Worker – Children with Disabilities as well as the information guide called *Children with disabilities and special needs – a parent's guide to services in Newcastle*. The research work was funded by the AMASE (Advanced Multi Agency Service Environment) project team of the University of Newcastle upon Tyne.

This guide and the research would not have been possible without the sustained commitment, help and enthusiasm of many people. As approximately 90 people have been involved throughout different phases of the work and research, we are unable to thank everyone individually.

We would like to thank the members of the steering group that met frequently and worked as a design team for the 'signposting' guide: Mary Kelly, Mandy Robinson and Kathy Rist. Thanks also to Newcastle Special Needs Network for their many contributions and to all the parents who informed the process, especially Caroline Field.

Thank you to Petrina Rowley and the NHS Direct (North East) Information Team for researching the information and producing the guide and to Debbie Oxberry and the Patient Information Centre Team for acting as a 'contact point' for parents and workers to request a copy of the guide.

Many parents and workers took part in the research by responding to the survey, being interviewed and participating in focus groups and we would like to thank them all. We are very grateful to Michelle Myers for the administrative support to the Development Worker and to Gillian Teesdale for acting as note-taker in the focus group and transcribing interviews and focus group tapes during the research phase.

Finally, one of the main findings and conclusion involves understanding the partnership that developed between the Development Worker and the Academic Researcher. Both feel that this has been very constructive and there are plans to write a short paper about the value of such partnership working in the government's agenda for joining up services. Val Bagnall and Bridgette Wessels both thank each other for the joys and struggles of genuine partnership working.

Bridgette Wessels and Val Bagnall

Notes on terminology

In the report the terms 'parent' and 'carer' are used interchangeably, and refer to all non-professionals who are involved in the care of a disabled child. Also, the terms 'professionals' and 'workers' are used interchangeably with both terms referencing those people who are involved in the care of a child in a professional capacity. As the authors are aware of the debates concerning terminology, in this report a lead is taken from some local parents and both the terms 'disabled children' and 'children with disabilities' are used.

There are many definitions of family, and the term is laden with (ideological) connotations. The authors have therefore produced a broad definition to be as value neutral as possible and to encompass as many configurations of family units as possible. In this report, the term family refers to 'family unit'. This is defined as a group of individuals who form an economic unit and social unit, and whose adult member(s) is/are responsible for the upbringing and welfare of children, and who share at some time a common residence or have shared a common residence at some point.

To maintain the anonymity of the survey respondents the authors have used the term s/he throughout the report.

Executive summary

In this report the authors explore the processes of producing a 'signposting' guide about local community services and the early use of the guide by carers and workers within the dynamics of the provision of services. The rationale for conducting this work is that both professionals and carers identify that there is a lack of well designed 'information' that meets the needs of carers, and which is also useful for professionals who work with carers and disabled children. This is especially problematic given the complex needs of disabled children and the equally complex world of service provision.

The complexities of enabling and supporting disabled children are reflected in 1) the social model of disability, which addresses the holistic needs of a child with impairments, and 2) as a corollary to this, the development of a multi-agency service to meet the needs of disabled children. This complexity is reflected in the provision of information. In Newcastle upon Tyne there are many statutory and voluntary organisations that provide information, but there was not (until the guide) *one* source of information for parents of disabled children about statutory and voluntary services or any clarity about what the range comprised of. One source of information about local services such as a guide is, generally speaking, taken to be helpful given the complexity of disability and the mixed economy of welfare in which carers construct coping strategies. Policy makers and a variety of professionals working in the field of services for disabled children and their carers identify a signposting guide

as a good starting point from which to build a more planned and systematic approach to information. This raises two main questions:

1) What should a signposting guide 'look like' and how should it be developed?
2) What are the dynamics of providing information in the context of carers of disabled children?

These questions serve to unpack some of the assumptions made about information (for example, that somehow information is 'good', is 'timely and relevant', and so on) and gain an understanding of what is involved in making information 'meaningful' and useful within the dynamics of family care and service provision.

The authors' conclusions are:

1) The guide is a useful 'signposting' resource of local services for parents.
2) There is a need to understand information within the service provision in which it is embedded.
3) The various contexts of use of information need to be understood in relation to the design of information.
4) Designing information needs to be understood as a process in which the development of relevant partnerships is central.
5) Finally, the guide is a good first step and its further development needs to remain within a multi-agency remit within a broader multi-agency strategy (for details see **Chapter six**).

Introduction

Understanding information in the context of parents of children with disabilities

In this report the authors consider the production and early use of an information guide for parents of children with disabilities. It focuses on the process of producing a 'signposting' guide to *local* services and the early use of the guide. Another dimension involves understanding the current thinking and practice of a variety of welfare and support services and how that environment interacts with the practice of producing and using information. To this end, the report considers the guide *Children with disabilities and special needs – a parent's guide to services in Newcastle* at the applied level with due consideration of the broader policy environment. Throughout the report the above named guide will simply be referred to as 'the guide'.

The report focuses on an information guide, the purpose of which is to provide basic information about local community services and to act as a signpost to other sources of more detailed information and support. The target group is parents of children with disabilities and special needs. Disability has many definitions and the authors adopt a 'social model' of disability (Morris, 1988; Oliver, 1999), which addresses the social and functional aspects of disability. The wider environment for the guide is comprised of the services and the professionals who work with families with disabled children. This is a complex area comprised of many professionals from different occupations in health, the local authority and the voluntary sector. Another development in Newcastle relevant to families, professionals and the provision of information is the development of multi-agency working around the needs of disabled children.

The overarching problem identified by information professionals and service practitioners is the lack of one point of access to information specifically for parents of disabled children. Parents identify with this problem and they commonly do not have access to relevant, timely and comprehensive information that affects the ways in which they can facilitate an independent and fulfilling life for their children. One issue that has arisen, as service provision is changing and the needs of parents are understood, is defining the role of information within the dynamics of family care and service provision. This involves understanding the characteristics of information in the disability-family-services context. The signposting guide was designed as a **step towards improving access to information and as a source of information for the emerging multi-agency services**.

Report outline

The aim of this report is to describe the grounded process of developing a guide, to evaluate its early use and to draw conclusions about the use of information in the current development of service provision in Newcastle upon Tyne.

Chapter two discusses the current policy and provision of services and information in relation to the needs of families with disabled children.

Chapter three outlines the rationale behind developing a 'signposting' guide and describes a practical working model for producing a guide.

Chapters four and **five** present the findings of research carried out to understand the ways in which the guide was received by parents of disabled children and by the professionals involved in the care of disabled children. **Chapter five** also provides detailed evidence about professionals' roles in providing information and working with other services, as well as the information they find of greatest use.

In **Chapter six**, the conclusion outlines the main findings of the project and the research into the use of the guide and their significance. The chapter also highlights good practice for producing a guide to services. This is followed by recommendations for policy and further research questions in **Chapter seven**.

Understanding information

This section of the report discusses the current policy and provision of services in relation to the needs of families with disabled children. The contents of this section of the report are:

- policy context;
- broad research context: national and local.

Policy context

There are several factors that are relevant to the development of information resources and their use in the context of parents and carers of disabled children. These are the nature of welfare provision, policies pertaining to aspects of childcare and disability and the experiences of parents/carers of disabled children. The four main trends that impact on the provision of information are: 1) the rethinking of service provision based on user choice; 2) the continuous reorganisation of welfare via new emerging forms of public sector management; 3) the development of a social model of disability and the government's social exclusion agenda; and 4) parents' experience of current service provision as being fragmented. Each of these trends is discussed briefly to provide a context for understanding the development of the guide in the current service–information–carer environment.

A major change in the provision of welfare from the 1980s onwards is the orientation of service users exercising choice. Coinciding with this orientation are the ongoing changes of management in the public sector. In general terms the organisation of welfare moved away from traditional forms of state-run authoritative bureaucracy to adoptions of private sector techniques based on various types of service contracts. A consequence of this is the fragmentation of traditional forms of welfare, and to counter this fragmentation there is currently a drive for services to form partnerships (Walsh, 1995).

Both of these interrelated trends have contributed to service users experiencing welfare services as complex and disjointed and have led service providers to plan for and form 'partnerships' so that they can provide a more coherent service. A corollary to this is the issue of enabling parents to make choices in regard to welfare provision. For services to be based on user choice, users need information so that they can act as 'informed consumers'. This has brought to the attention of policy makers and service users, issues surrounding the provision of information in welfare services (see **Cited research**, page 78, University of York, 2002-02; Norah Fry Research Centre, 1999-2002).

Thus, this combination of choice, a partially fragmented and an emerging partnership service sector means that service users need information to be able to navigate the field of welfare provision and then to construct the service they need. Information has the potential to enable users to demand the type and quality of services they want. However, both the provision of information by service providers and the use of information by parents are complex. The nature and provision of information, therefore, needs to be addressed to ensure that service users are able to exercise choice and in so doing render service providers accountable.

Another aspect of the rethinking of welfare in relation to service partnerships and the needs of service users is that welfare 'problems' cannot be understood simply in terms of one dimension. Thus, for example, a medical definition of a child's impairment involves understanding the broader situation of a child 'being disabled', which is complex and involves many dimensions including health, financial implications, housing, schooling, family and social life. The government's Social Exclusion agenda aims to address the multidimensionality of health and welfare issues. Working to this agenda, government is encouraging the 'joining up of services' to meet the needs of individuals, groups and families. An important aspect of joining up services is the provision of information across agencies and professionals, as well as between services and service users. These general trends in welfare provision suggest that information is an important aspect of service provision. Information for service users will enable them to become 'informed consumers'. In addition, service providers need information to coordinate provision in emerging service partnerships and forms of multi-agency working.

Simultaneously there has been a renaissance in childcare policy and a focus on disability issues. The renaissance of childcare policy developed through a combination of political factors and societal pressures, as well as a general dissatisfaction with the management of cases of presumed child abuse. The social, political and economic context of providing services to children is ultimately set within broader cultural values of the 'rights of the child' as seen, for example, in the United Nations Convention on the Rights of the Child. The development and characteristics of children's services situate the 'child' and his or her needs at the centre of any service provision (Foley et al, 2001, p 1). The government believed that a fundamental review was required, which included addressing a perceived lack of involvement by parents in decision making about their children; the government also recognised that children's feelings and wishes were seldom taken into consideration (Foley et al, 2001). Within this context, the 1989 Children Act became law in England and Wales. The promotion of Children Services Planning Groups has also encouraged, among a number of foci, a focus on the needs of children with disabilities and complex health needs.

There is no single 'correct' definition of disability: the definition used within the 1989 Children Act describes substantial and permanent disability, but different services use different definitions. However, helpful to our understanding of information in the context of parents with disabled children is the move (made by the disability movement and some professionals) from an individual to a social model of disability (Marchant, 2001). The social model of disability does not use the term 'disability' to refer to impairment in the narrow sense of functional limitations, but rather to describe the effects of prejudice and discrimination, the social factors that create barriers, deny opportunities and thereby dis-able people (Morris, 1998; Oliver, 1999). The social context of childhood disability is one that *excludes* disabled children in many different ways from everyday life. Disabled children are often very vulnerable in our society and experience many forms of oppression (Middleton, 1996), and disabled children and adults often experience discrimination in healthcare (Rutter and Seyman, 1999). Current research and policy stresses that although disabled children's needs might be more complex, take more time or continue for more of childhood, basic care nonetheless remains a right of all children (Marchant, 2001).

The social definition of disability is influential in raising issues in the ways services are delivered and how they also relate to parents' expectations for their children. This is because the definition stresses the complex ways in which disability can produce social exclusion. To this end, much of multi-agency service aims to support children and families in the community. In addition, parents want their children to have the opportunity to participate in a range of activities that interest their children and help them to develop (Thomson, 2000). Addressing the exclusionary aspects of disability is complex because parents feel that children with disabilities need some specialist support but that this should not prevent children from participating more generally in social life. This balance between inclusion and exclusion, between specialist support and general participation has implications for the design of information provision. The provision of information needs to be designed to support the aspirations that parents have for their children and to be appropriate to the nature of the support services. Information (and services) needs to be inclusive, but must also address the specialist needs of this group without stigmatising them.

Services for disabled children tend to be fragmented between different agencies. Disabled children often come sequentially to the attention of health, then education and then social workers (Marchant, 2001). Different perspectives, values and professional languages can complicate working together across agency and discipline boundaries. This not only affects the self-esteem and identity of disabled children, but it also affects the ways in which families and carers can care for their children. Some families describe dealing with service providers as being the most difficult aspect of caring for their disabled children (DoH, 1998). Some of these difficulties arise because of a lack of clarity about the roles and responsibilities of professionals and services (Twig and Atkin,

two

1993). For many parents and carers, therefore, the service environment is complex and confusing. In this context, information about different services may help parents to manage their situation.

The above gives the broad context in which a parent's guide to services was developed and produced. The guide is called *Children with disabilities and special needs – a parent's guide to services in Newcastle*. The policy context indicates that parents need information to access services. They need information to make choices about care and they need information to navigate and negotiate what is often a complex and disjointed provision of service. There is, however, an assumption that information can enable parents to make choices about what services they want for their child and that services become accountable through parents exercising choice by being informed consumers. However, this assumption needs to be understood more clearly because studies from the perspectives of families with children with disabilities show that the above policies are not, as yet, helping parents. There is also a lack of appropriate information to support parents managing partnerships of care and care packages (Beresford, 1995; Sloper, 1999). Studies show that gaining access to information is problematic for many carers and that the provision of information is, at present, inadequate to ensure that carers can facilitate the appropriate support for their disabled children.

Studies suggest that access to quality information given in an appropriate way may well help the welfare of disabled children and their carers. However, many studies of parents with disabled children report that parents find it difficult to get information and the subsequent lack of awareness often means that parents do not get the support they need to ensure that their child leads an independent and fulfilling life. The next section summarises some of these studies and their findings.

Broad research context: national and local

While the above changes in policy were (and still are) occurring, studies of families with disabled children show the difficulties that many families experience in accessing information and services. Research on the needs of families with disabled children has produced consistent findings. These cover a range of time periods and areas together with a variety of populations, such as families of children with learning disabilities and/or physical disabilities as well as from different ethnic groups. Sloper (1999) points out that the message from these studies is that substantial numbers of families report a 'constant battle' to find out:

- what services are available;
- the different roles of different agencies and different professionals;
- to get professionals to understand their situation and their needs;
- to obtain recognition of their own knowledge of their child;
- to negotiate delays and bureaucracy.

A consequence of this is that there are high levels of unmet needs. These include information about services, the child's condition, how to help the child and about practical support with housing, finance and transport, and breaks from care (Mukherjee et al, 1999).

This has been recognised at policy level. Quality Protects, for example, highlights and re-emphasises the importance and role of information for parents of disabled children that many local and national studies show. Therefore sub-objective 6-4 of Quality Protects is:

> To ensure that parents and disabled children are provided with information about services from the statutory and voluntary sector on an interagency basis.

The studies described later highlight aspects of the difficulties many parents' experience. Before considering these, Beresford (1995) in *Expert opinions: A survey of parents caring for a severely disabled child* recognised that many parents:

> ... found collecting information about their child's condition was an important aspect of coping with emotional distress and also put them in a better position to demand the level of service to which their child was entitled. (p 34)

The ease of that process needs to be understood to help ascertain whether parents do have access to timely and relevant information, in ways that do not add extra stress to an already sensitive and difficult time for parents. Knox (1995) explored families' needs for information and other forms of support. The comments by parents talking about welfare benefits typify experiences of finding out about services:

> "Nothing was said about benefits or disability at the hospital, so I didn't think we were entitled to anything."

> "If you don't know, how can you ask?"

Knox (1995) pointed out that parents need to know that information, advice and support services exist. Many parents have said that they 'find out (about) information in passing' from other parents; that they have to do their own research for information; and that they often miss out on services for years due to lack of information. In these contexts 'people', including other parents/carers and workers, were seen to be the key to information. Information is widely recognised as a key to helping disabled people and their carers improve the quality of their own lives and for them to be able to make choices and have control over their own lives. Knox argues that many families with disabled children find information difficult to access and find the system of provision complex with many not aware of what is available. This undermines their ability to gain control and exercise choice to improve their own and their child's quality of life.

two

Further work by the Joseph Rowntree Foundation (Mitchell and Sloper, 2000) and Knox (1997) identifies the type of information needed by parents:

- what the services are and the range of services in statutory and voluntary sectors, for example, childcare and short breaks, leisure activities, housing adaptations, support groups, and so on;
- what the services do;
- where to go and how to get help in a crisis;
- who's who in services and the roles of workers and where to find them;
- access to services, eligibility criteria;
- times of change and key periods in child's life, for example, starting school, changing schools, planning to leave school, moving on to adult services;
- benefits entitlement;
- rights and complaints procedures.

Local practice-based research in Newcastle upon Tyne shows that many parents get information from the following sources:

- word of mouth/people/workers;
- telephone helplines;
- written information;
- videos;
- audio tapes;
- Typetalk and Textphones;
- British Sign Language, symbols, etc;
- electronic information systems, Internet.

Local studies validate the findings of national studies showing the difficulties that parents have in trying to get information that is timely and relevant. For example, research from Contact a Family and Newcastle Special Needs Network (2000) *Have your say day*, found that one of the most trying issues for parents is being able to obtain information on the services available and what they are entitled to. Parents said:

> "It is so time consuming to get information about the services that are on offer."

> "Sometimes it feels like a conspiracy, that if families are told about services then they will immediately want to access them."

> "As parents we are always made to feel like pests, always asking for information when all we want is what we are entitled to for our children."

These comments highlight the practical difficulties that many parents face in trying to get information. They show that some parents do not trust services and they feel that services are not there to meet their needs. These perceptions are also echoed in relation to the roles of professionals in service provision. Knox (1997), for example, points out that many parents felt that workers sometimes controlled information and often did not give them the full picture. Knox argues that this could restrict choice and reinforce a parent's lack of control. In relation to this point, parents said:

> "It's no use (professionals) just handing over the booklet, [they need to] point out useful information to families."

"There needs to be training for workers in information-giving skills."

Davis (1993) further validates these comments, reporting that professionals frequently provide too little information or do not provide it at the right time or in an appropriate way. Parents want professionals to listen to them and to acknowledge their own expertise as parents. And parents request the sharing of information and 'negotiation' so that they are involved in decision making.

Families really appreciate it when professionals know how to use information. For example, in Contact a Family and Newcastle Special Needs Network (2000), one parent said:

> "My pre-schoolteacher was supportive, kind and knowledgeable about other services so she acted as a link person."

This comment shows the ways in which information, correctly provided and easily accessible, can help parents to negotiate services. Roberts and Lawton (2000) found that many families do not have a single point of access information source and that they are ill-informed and as a result find it harder to access services. The combination of these points shows how difficult it can be for parents to participate in shaping the care of their children.

The above scenario is further compounded by the complexity of the needs of families with children with disabilities and the multidimensionality of their needs. This complexity suggests that coordination of services needs to occur to meet the needs of parents and children. Parents who do not have access to information are less likely to be aware of what services are available and may not have access to information that would help them to coordinate services to manage their child's condition and their family situation. Due to this complexity, Roberts and Lawton (2000) point out that single points of access to information are very important to families, parents and carers. These 'single points of access to information sources' can take many forms, for example, voluntary organisations, child development centres, multi-agency information resources and information guides.

Roberts and Lawton (2000) argue that a comparative evaluation of how useful families may find these sources is needed. This report goes some way to addressing part of that by considering the **design, production and early use** of an information guide in the context of Newcastle from the perspectives of parents and professionals. It also considers the guide in the **current policy environment and the needs of families**, so addressing some of the issues of situating information within service dynamics. This combination of situating the design of information in service and user dynamics will help us to understand further what the appropriate design of information packages for parents of disabled children might be.

two

Children with disabilities and special needs

a parent's guide

to services in Newcastle

December 2000

Developing a guide to services

This part of the report outlines the rationale behind developing a signposting guide to *local* services in Newcastle upon Tyne and describes a practical working model that could be adapted in other areas of the country and for other types of services.

Throughout this section, the health and social services funded 'Development Worker – Children with Disabilities' is simply referred to as the Development Worker.

The contents of this section are:

- Why develop a guide to services for parents of disabled children?;
- Lessons learned from elsewhere (October–December 1999);
- The development phase (February– September 2000);
- Increasing the ways parents can access information about services;
- The guide specification and the work starts (September 2000);
- The last lap! (November 2000–February 2001);
- How would parents and workers know about the guide?;
- Multidisciplinary workshops (February and March 2001);
- Working in partnership with the Patient Information Centre (PIC).

Why a guide to services for parents of disabled children?

Locally, there were many statutory and voluntary organisations providing different types of information. There was no *one* source of information listing both statutory and voluntary sector services or any clarity about what the range comprised of. At the time, there were no plans by any other agency for a similar local guide, so there would be no duplication.

Parents want and need to know what services exist in their area and how and where to make the initial contact. Their experiences of 'how' they find out about the type of help available shows that they may or may not 'hit on' information to give them the initial 'way in' to services.

The guide is intended to provide basic information about community services and act as a signpost to other sources of more detailed information and support available locally. It lists many of the services from health, local authority and voluntary organisations. The contact details are given for each of the services, as well as opening times and if a parent can contact the service directly or if a referral is necessary.

It was understood that the guide would not meet all information needs of parents: for example, it does not list services and groups that have a 'national' base. To do so would have meant that the guide would have been extremely lengthy. However, the contact details of organisations that can signpost to the wealth of national information are given in the guide. Parents need a range of different types of information in different formats, from in-depth booklets to leaflets, videos and websites. Different ways of accessing information is also needed via, for example, the telephone, Internet and face-to-face contact.

As well as providing parents with the information they said they needed, the development of the guide would 'kick-start' the process of looking afresh at a more planned and systematic approach to information provision. Lessons learned from the process of developing the guide and the feedback from parents (and workers) about its usefulness will assist and give some direction to developing a multi-agency strategy for a package of different types of information. It would also identify areas of unmet need and areas of further research.

Although the guide was developed primarily for parents, it was acknowledged that its production could be of value to service planners and providers, as follows:

- Listing key statutory and voluntary services, in other words a 'mapping' of local statutory and voluntary services. There was general agreement that it was difficult for everyone (parents and services) to see a 'whole picture' of services.

- The information about services was not easily available to the range of information providers in Newcastle, for example, the Children's Information Service and the Carers Information Point. NHS Direct (North East) were commissioned to produce the guide and their Health Information Manager later commented that researching and collating the information (which many people refer to as 'specialist') greatly informed their ability to respond to parents and professionals contacting their service.

- The guide will provide the Task Group for Children with Disabilities (part of Newcastle's Children Services Planning Mechanism) with a clearer picture of groups and organisations to approach and involve when planning and taking forward specific pieces of work.

- The timeliness of the production of the guide. For example, the formation of the new Children with Disabilities Team of social workers and nurses, and the organisational changes taking place in many of the statutory services.

- Workers have also identified their own need for this type of information. It was hoped that the guide would provide a useful tool in the relationship with families, so that together it will be easier for parents to find their way around the maze of services.

- Education and training in 'information giving' – the guide can be used as a local resource as part of the training courses and induction sessions of local organisations.

Lessons learned from elsewhere

As development workers are natural resource and information investigators, the starting point in Newcastle upon Tyne, when considering the practical aspects of developing a 'guide to services,' was to find out what had happened in other parts of the country where similar guides or directories of services have been produced. Learning from the literature was also important, as **Chapter two** of this report has outlined.

Over a period of two months involving a telephone and e-mail chase around the country, the Development Worker built up a picture of the different types of feedback available. This feedback from parents and workers from, for example Kingston upon Hull, Wrexham and Somerset, was very positive about the usefulness of 'signposting' guides. Eight sample directories were collected and comparisons were made about the size, title, use of language, font size, organisation of the information and special features, to see if this would give guidance for the work in Newcastle upon Tyne.

Comparisons

- There is no single preferred **size of publication** and they ranged from A5 spiral bound (155 pages) to A4 stapled soft-backed booklet (44 pages). The average number of pages was 132, although the geographical area for some was a region rather than one local authority area.
- While some parents do have **language preferences**, for example, parents in

Somerset did not wish to see 'disability' in the title, others say they are more interested in having the information than becoming too 'bogged down' with concerns about language.
- There were differences in the way the **sections of information** were organised, for example, some by age and others by listed organisation.
- Each directory has its **own style and special features**, ranging from: explanations of roles of professionals, glossary of terms, maps, graphics, colour, cross-referencing and comprehensive indexing, 'personal' information page, to inclusion of 'update' sheets.

Evaluation of the usefulness of the guides

The informal and formal information available concerning evaluation of the guides was also carefully considered. For example, the key findings from consultation meetings with parents (Somerset Impact, 1998) show:

- Parents felt 'the book' should be given to all families of children of all ages and stages in assessment and diagnosis.
- Parents expected professionals from all agencies to know about the book and to be able to learn from them what was in it and together to find the relevant information.
- Parents agreed that a 'book' will never replace face-to-face contact and should ideally be handed out by someone close to the family who can help parents make the best use of it.
- The 'book' needs to be clear, concise, simple and user friendly.

three

Summary of lessons learned from elsewhere

Having looked at the experiences of other areas producing guides or directories, the following conclusions were made by the Development Worker:

1) Comparing sample guides/directories showed that there is no single commonly used 'template' and this emphasises the importance of understanding the local needs of parents to inform 'process'.

2) There has to be absolute clarity about the aim of any information designed for parents, signposting information cannot address all the different information needs of individual parents.

3) It is impossible to include all services in one user-friendly guide, so the information needs to give parents the 'starting point' and where to go for further, more detailed information.

4) You will never please everyone ... you will never win ... and mistakes will happen!

5) It takes far longer to research, develop and produce the information in a 'directory' format than people think. There is a fine balance between taking time to ensure that all the different stages are carried out appropriately and not taking too long so that the information becomes increasingly out of date.

6) The task is complex and requires a specialist set of skills. One year was quoted as the absolute minimum amount of time needed.

7) Information is constantly changing, and even when 'hot off the press' some of the information will inevitably have been overtaken by change.

8) Aiming to have annually updated versions of guides is unrealistic and new editions are not simply updating the information in the existing version.

9) Directories and guides need to evolve to reflect the changing look of services and legislation. Amendments and additions will also be identified as part of the feedback and evaluation process.

10) Some areas have dropped the use of 'ring binders' after discovering that providing 'update sheets' is not a workable option.

11) Parents' involvement is paramount, however, parents do have different views and preferences and no one publication will be able to incorporate all of these, therefore 'hard decisions' have to be made.

It was at the end of this first stage in the process that the Development Worker concluded there might be value in recording in the form of a 'working model' the whole process of developing a guide to services. This would hopefully provide other areas with a more informed starting point for their own local resource and minimise the time they may spend 'chasing around the country' to understand the lessons learned from elsewhere.

The development phase

The steering group

The next part of the process was the setting up of a steering group, which began meeting on a regular basis in February 2000. The main task of the group was to develop a 'guide specification' for use by a commissioned organisation that would produce the actual guide. The group of five included a local parent and workers from voluntary and statutory organisations. The Development Worker facilitated the planning meetings. The group's membership comprised people experienced in information provision as well as having considerable experience of direct work with families of disabled children.

Parents' views and involvement, the lessons learned from elsewhere, the literature and local studies in Newcastle upon Tyne informed all of the work of the steering group.

Principles, issues and work of the steering group

The following is the agenda of work identified by the steering group:

1) To ensure that parents and appropriate workers are involved at each and every stage of the work, for example, parents' focus groups with an independent facilitator. Focus group members could also act as reference points at other stages of the work.
2) The content and look of the document to be guided by parents and any local good practice guidelines.
3) To consider the 'look' of the guide: format, style, language, typeface, graphics, colour, and so on.
4) Identify the ways of linking families to information; for example, to ask parents for guidance about unsolicited direct mailing and to explore the possible use of 'registers' in Newcastle as a medium for mailings.
5) Work with others to develop and deliver a publicity and distribution strategy.
6) Ensure that systems are set up for monitoring the number of parents and others requesting a guide.
7) Explore and identify the ways of obtaining feedback about the usefulness of the guide that would then inform any further information developments.

Early in the life of the steering group's work, the parent member of the group withdrew. This was due to family commitments that required her to leave the country for a period of time. Although many efforts were made to attract another parent, no one else was able to be involved.

However, many other parents were involved throughout all the phases of the work, from the development phase (February-September 2000), the six multidisciplinary workshops (February-March 2001) and finally during the research and evaluation phase (April-June 2001).

three

15

Parental involvement

The following lists the ways parents contributed:

- Individual meetings with the Development Worker and three parents on a one-to-one basis to talk about their information needs and ways of finding information.
- A parent was a member of the steering group throughout the early stage of the work.
- Views and contributions were invited via newsletters and several parents' meetings of, for example, a parent-led network called the Newcastle Special Needs Network (NSNN).
- The three parent members of the Task Group for Children with Disabilities.
- An independently facilitated focus group (March 2000).
- Sharing and using the collective experience of each member of the steering group of working with and listening to parent's thoughts and views about information.

A second focus group of parents was also planned in one of the 'additionally resourced' units in a mainstream school. However, there was very little response to personal invitations to parents to take part and the group did not go ahead. The school itself had been very enthusiastic about being involved, as the teachers wanted to be more responsive to parents' information needs.

The steering group was reminded that the pressures that parents experience can be a **barrier to participation in service development** and understanding ways of enabling more parents to become involved is an area for further work. However, the steering group felt confident that the views of parents had been gathered in a variety of ways and that there was unanimous agreement by parents as to what was needed; the following box summarises the guidance from parents.

> **Parents views on what the guide should be like**
>
> - The information should 'signpost' to organisations and further sources of information rather than attempt to be a complete listing of all organisations for every condition and disability.
> - The information should be user friendly and concise and be easy to photocopy.
> - The guide should be made available to workers as a tool in their information role with parents.
> - The guide should be kept simple and in as many formats as possible. Although some parents actively access information via the Internet, parents felt 'paper copy' is still the most commonly used information resource.

There was a consensus in the focus group that society is becoming 'too politically correct' about the use of language and that the terms 'disabled' and 'disability' need not be negative terms. They felt that the 'tone' of the publication was probably more important than the language used. This was very helpful to the steering group, as there had been a great deal of discussion about, for example, a 'title' for the guide that would be acceptable to parents and not serve to alienate them.

Common themes about information and services identified by parents throughout the developmental phase of the work

Listening to and working with parents identified very similar issues and concerns about information and their relationship with services, as local and national studies have previously reported. A summary of some of the main findings is found in **Chapter two**. There was a sense of parents having to 'battle' to be heard and be given information. This was often their initial experience and a repeated experience as the children reached each stage in their development. Parents said they had no way of knowing 'which' workers provide help to families of disabled children and exactly what their individual roles are. There is a common feeling among parents of having to seek information themselves, as the following comments from the parents' focus group show:

"You do not know where to start, I went to the library and that was no help."

"Without information, help and support is delayed and difficult to access."

"I don't know what I would have done without the information my neighbour gave me."

The parents further said about workers:

"They [professionals] need education themselves, they lack knowledge about the services available."

"There is poor communication between hospitals and community services ... they think in straight lines."

Finding an organisation with the skills to produce a quality guide

The steering group debated the lessons learned from other areas (described on pages 13-14, **Lessons learned from elsewhere**); particularly noting "the task is complex and requires specialist skills". It was then agreed that an organisation was needed that was well placed to research and produce a quality guide, and that could ideally also offer 'something extra' that would be helpful to parents when they are looking for information.

three

It was felt that NHS Direct in the North East could provide such a comprehensive service with 'added value', and for the following reasons:

• NHS Direct (North East Ambulance NHS Trust) has considerable experience of researching and producing health and social care directories and was able to undertake all the different components of the work. This ranged from researching, collating and organising all the information, to structuring, having the guide designed/printed and 'delivering boxes to the door'. Their ability to do this would reduce the amount of time taken to produce the guide.

• All the information collected for the guide would become a routine part of the NHS Direct (North East) core database that is maintained and updated on a regular basis. This database is also purchased and used by a number of other information providers throughout the city.

Increasing the ways parents can access information about services

The 'added value' of using NHS Direct is that parents (and workers) now have an **increased range of ways of obtaining information** about services for children with disabilities. Having more than one way to access information (in this case a hard copy 'guide') is a theme that runs through all the local and national research and was reiterated by the local parents' focus group. The information subsequently researched for the guide has

the potential to reach a much larger audience via the following:

• NHS Direct (24-hour service) via the helpline, Textphone and Typetalk facilities and the 24-hour 'Language Line'.
• Face-to-face contact of parents (and others) with information providers using the NHS Direct database.
• Touch screen health information points (HIP) at a local supermarket, the West End Resource Centre, three medical centres, two pharmacies and GOSIP (General On Street Information Point) in the city centre.

The steering group went on to look at other ways to have the information in the guide as accessible as possible within the constraints of the budget. There were discussions with experienced information providers and the communications departments of statutory organisations, as well as reference to good practice guidelines such as the Community Care Information Project (1998) *Making information accessible, good practice guide*.

The following was explored and agreed by the steering group.

Large print

The Royal National Institute for the Blind (see RNIB, 2001) recommends that large print is a minimum of 14- to 16-point (type sizes) for visually impaired people. The guide is available in A4 size and 14-point sans serif typeface (more accessible to readers with visual difficulties). An enlargement to A3 is easily arranged.

Audio tapes

This is not appropriate due to the 'directory' style of information; very important features of using the guide are the 'index' and 'contents' sections as well as the ability to browse through the various sections.

Braille

The guide has been transcribed into Braille and further copies can be produced within a period of days.

Typetalk and Textphone

The leaflets and posters advertising the 'contact' organisation for copies of the guide also informed parents of the organisation's Typetalk and Textphone facilities.

Computers and the Internet

Parents in the focus group recommended that a 'paper guide' would be the best medium for the information. However, they recognised that many parents and workers use electronic methods to find information. The guide is available in PDF format and work is underway exploring the best use of this. The guide has been posted on the city council Intranet site and there is interest from a number of organisations that have websites.

What about parents whose first language is not English?

The constraint on the budget was that it was not possible to have the guide translated into a wide range of community languages. The steering group was also confused about the usefulness or otherwise of such an approach and recognised its own limitations in understanding appropriate ways for people whose preferred language is not English to access information. Although the group felt that this is an area for further local research, it was hoped that the following would at least offer some options for parents:

- NHS Direct (North East) provides a service called 'Language Line'. This is a telephone interpreting service (24 hours, seven days a week) in over 100 languages. Members of the public wishing to use Language Line to find out about services for children with disabilities can do so by ringing NHS Direct (telephone 0845 4647) and saying which language they would prefer to use. Apart from the cost of the local telephone call, there is no charge for the service and callers can give their preference for either a male or female interpreter.
- 'Link workers' – many of the services listed in the directory, *Services available in Newcastle for people from black and ethnic groups*, compiled by the Patient Information Centre in 2002, were sent a sample of the guide. For example, Dekh Bhal Asian Carers Project. An information sheet describing the 'Language Line' service of NHS Direct accompanied this. It was hoped that the link workers would be able to help families access the information.

three

The guide specification and starting the work

The steering group completed the development phase of the work during the summer of 2000 and the following describes the 'guide specification' that was produced for the commissioned organisation. The specification, particularly the checklist of tasks and the design specification, can be easily adapted and used in other areas interested in producing a similar information guide.

The guide specification

1) To identify and research details of all key local services in the statutory and voluntary sectors, collate and organise the information into a hard copy directory format, design and print 3,000 guides to be delivered to an agreed location.

2) To design and print complementary leaflets and posters for parents describing the guide and giving information on how to receive a copy.

3) The timescale for the work to be completed was within four months.

Principles

The guide should:

- follow good practice guidelines concerning information provision and accessibility such as Community Care Information Project (1998) *Making information accessible, good practice guide*;
- be user friendly, easy to read and use;
- be jargon free, clear and concise, written with members of the public in mind;
- avoid relying on abbreviations alone;
- contain sufficient information in each of the entries to trigger a response and avoid being so detailed that the volume of information disempowers parents;
- identify the date the information was collected;
- not make assumptions about the level of knowledge parents have about both service provision and the roles of key professionals.

Process

At each stage in the development of the guide there will be ongoing liaison and meetings between the commissioned organisation and the Development Worker to ensure good communication and decision making.

This will enable the **commissioned organisation** to:

- obtain any clarification needed;
- provide the Development Worker with suggestions and options, for example, on structure and design;
- advise on progress, provide 'drafts' for comments and amendments before going to print.

Tasks checklist

1) Identify and research information about all local key services in the statutory and voluntary sectors, for example, within health, social services, housing, leisure and education. For this guide it was signposting information to key services in the community available for families of disabled children living in the local authority area of Newcastle upon Tyne.

2) Liaise with each identified organisation to obtain accurate and up to date information concerning:
   - The 'contact' details, including the name of the organisation, telephone, fax and minicom numbers, and e-mail and website addresses.
   - The role of the organisation and a description of the type of services provided.
   - The 'opening' times, 'referral procedures', who can use the service and any service costs.
   - Any other information felt to be appropriate.

3) Collate the information.

4) Advise the Development Worker on options for organising the information; for example, by age group, topic area (short breaks, benefits, adaptations, etc), type of organisation or other suggestions.

5) Organise the information into sections including a brief introduction to each section.

6) Ensure the drafts are proofread by a minimum of four people.

Appearance

The guide should:

1) Be a maximum of 60 pages in total, less if possible.

2) Be A4 in size, wiro-bound, white pages (matt finish) with black print.

3) Combine text with the use of some symbols; for example, telephone symbol and graphics, possibly at the beginning of each new section.

4) Use point size 14 for main body of text, larger point size where appropriate.

5) Have a front cover which is eye-catching and colourful (two colours) with title and date.

6) Include an introduction and 'how to use the guide' section as well as a 'welcome'. In this guide, from a parent and from the chair of the Task Group for Children with Disabilities.

7) Contain a 'contents' section, plus an 'introduction' to each section.

8) Include a comprehensive, well cross-referenced index.

9) Give explanations of terms used, brief descriptions of roles of key professionals.

10) List contact details of at least two information providers for information not given in the guide; for example, national organisations and for 'further information'.

11) Include a self-completion questionnaire.

three

The work begins

Using the previous specification, the commissioned organisation began the research and information collation in September 2000. It maintained regular contact with the steering group both to update and to request appropriate guidance and decision making via the Development Worker.

The last lap!

After three months of research and collation of information, the 'draft' stage for the guide and publicity materials was reached by late November 2000. There began a very intensive and critical period of work. For the commissioned organisation it was a continuation of a great deal of focused and detailed work. The Development Worker was now very involved, often liaising on a daily basis with the steering group members and many other people invited to contribute. The Development Worker also had to ensure that the commissioned organisation received clear and detailed feedback.

Practicalities at the draft stage

It was not possible to incorporate all of the parents' suggestions or in fact, everything in the specification. For example, it was planned to include graphics throughout the guide. To do this would have meant sacrificing pages of information about services and the steering group felt the information would be more important to parents than the graphics. It was disappointing that it was not possible to have symbols instead of wording for the different 'methods of contact', other than the telephone symbol that appears throughout the guide. The designer was not able to provide clear enough symbols for 'fax', 'Textphone', 'e-mail' and 'web addresses' of the required size. The decision was that to include the symbols could have caused confusion instead of making the guide easier to use.

One parent had suggested different coloured pages or coloured section dividers. Neither of these was possible due to financial constraints and the steering group was keen to see how important this sort of detail is to parents via the feedback work planned.

A draft of the guide was available in late November 2000 and contained the core of information concerning services, but without the design element. The index, contents and introductions to sections were added later. Draft copies were circulated to 20-30 people:

* directory steering group;
* Task Group for Children with Disabilities (including the three parent members);
* Newcastle Special Needs Network.

These represent a very wide range of people from parents to voluntary organisations to local authority and health trusts (both managers and workers delivering services).

Feedback was requested concerning:

- accuracy of the contact details and information;
- the 'contents' list and the order of sections;
- any obvious omissions;
- general comments on the 'feel' of the guide;
- ease of reading.

There was an extremely tight timescale to keep to, partly because printers close down for two weeks over the Christmas period, but primarily due to concerns about information becoming out of date quickly. New information and legislation is becoming available all the time, as well as changes occurring in the services themselves. Without a strict timetable it is easy to see that the guide may never have been finished!

Responses

The eight people who responded provided extremely valuable help. Their feedback consisted of suggestions for amendments and additions as well as some restructuring of sections and changes to the content of two sections. One parent provided very detailed feedback about the guide, all of which helped to make the guide more 'user friendly' and appropriate. This parent continued to spend large chunks of her time contributing as she commented on the second draft as well as on the design/ colours of the cover and publicity materials. She also provided some comments for the 'introduction page' of the guide.

What happened next?

At the end of November 2000, the people who had been asked to comment on the first draft of the guide were sent an update about the many changes already made and those in the pipeline; for example, the section called 'breaks from caring' was being completely redone. The second draft was available by the second week in December and sent to the steering group and NSNN. After some necessary 'pruning' of entries (the guide needed to be a specific number of pages), the commissioned organisation arranged the proofreading and the guide went to the designers and printers. There were 3,000 in general release one month later.

What we learned

It was understood that it would be important to have a link person facilitating the process throughout all the phases of the work of developing a guide to services in Newcastle upon Tyne. Locally, it was the interagency Development Worker who was in a good position to take on this role. This was partly due to the traditional skills of development workers and partly due to the joint-funded nature of the post enabling an easier route to a variety of organisations and professionals. Added to this, the Development Worker's knowledge about information and many of the services assisted the commissioned organisation. However, it was underestimated how time consuming this would be! For example, from the beginning of 'draft guide stage' through to the initial distribution and coordination of the publicity strategy (November 2000-February 2001), the work needed to be a real priority within the overall workload of the Development Worker. The Development Worker was reminded of the 'lessons learned from elsewhere' outlined earlier in this section of the report; that "the task is complex and requires specialist sets of skills" and, "one year is the absolute minimum amount of time needed".

The following also became clearer at this stage:

- The many months of the steering groups' development work successfully produced the type of clear and detailed specification needed by any organisation being commissioned to produce a guide.
- The size of the steering group and the mix of skills had been 'just right'.
- It is essential to have a very good working relationship and communication system with the commissioned organisation. Without this, the many challenges could have become problems and barriers. This would have caused delays with the information collected becoming increasingly out of date.
- It is worthwhile involving a wide range of people at the draft stage, although their response time must be kept very short. Many of the people who were sent a draft copy of the guide were unable to respond, not because of lack of interest but due to constraints on their time.
- There were some suggestions made for inclusion of the type of information that was not within the scope of a signposting guide and would require for example, detailed information sheets about individual topics. A record needs to be kept of such suggestions so that other information needs of parents are addressed at a later date.

How would parents and workers know about the guide?

In the focus group in the developmental phase of the work, parents said that *they* wanted to make the decision about whether they had a copy of the guide. They suggested leaflets and posters, word of mouth and media work to publicise a 'contact' telephone number. Parents could then decide if they wanted to ring for a copy, rather than being handed one or sent one 'cold'. Ten thousand leaflets and 1,000 posters were subsequently printed and distributed. Some parents in other parts of the country take a different view; for example, in Somerset parents thought their 'book' should be "given to all families of disabled children".

A number of different ways of linking families to information was explored by the steering group. It was noted that in the future when Newcastle does have a robust health and social services register, it would be possible to send each family a leaflet telling them about the guide as well as other types of information. Even if this approach had been possible, the steering group felt that a variety of different ways of publicising the guide was still necessary.

The Newcastle and North Tyneside public relations (PR) group (comprising NHS and local authority workers) helped to inform the steering group's publicity strategy.

The publicity about the guide was targeted at the following groups.

Parents and families

The methods used were:

- The PR group utilised their local media contacts and there were articles about the guide in three free papers (*Health Today, City News and Herald* and *Post*) *delivered to every home* in the local authority area of Newcastle upon Tyne. Articles in local and regional daily papers complemented these. There was also a broadcast about the guide on local radio.
- Distribution of leaflets and posters, for example, in libraries, community centres, leisure centres, schools and swimming baths.
- Articles and information pieces in many newsletters, for example, Newcastle Carers Project, Contact a Family and NSNN. Several schools included information about the guide in their routine 'letters home'.

Workers in their information giving role

The methods used were:

- The multidisciplinary workshops for professionals (described in the following section).
- Each of the 'entries' in the guide (organisations/groups) was sent a complimentary copy as well as a covering letter, sample publicity materials and an information sheet. The information sheet was designed to enlist support in publicising the guide and advised on how to obtain further publicity materials.

- Each worker within several health and local authority services was sent a complimentary copy and samples of publicity materials; for example, Special Educational Needs Co-ordinators (SENCOs), social workers and nurses in the Children with Disabilities Team.
- The information sheet was e-mailed to local authority staff and to community health workers.
- Articles in staff newsletters of many voluntary and statutory organisations.

A change of strategy

The initial feedback was that some parents did not seem confident about using the contact point to request their own copy of the guide. Although the parents' focus group had not suggested families be offered a guide directly, it was felt a change of strategy was necessary. In April 2001, the Development Worker arranged for boxes of guides to be distributed to specialist services; for example, Special Educational Needs Teaching and Support Services (SENTASS), Specialist School Health Nursing, Parent Partnership Officers (Education) and Children's Community Nursing Service. Voluntary organisations were also supplied with boxes; for example, the Carers Information Point and Disability North. This change of strategy was to enable services to offer a guide directly to parents.

three

Lessons learned

The first meeting to plan the publicity about the guide took place in September 2000 and allowed enough time (five months) to ensure that the many people who assisted during this period were clear about their role and contributions. It was one of many examples throughout the life of the guide's development of the voluntary and statutory sector effectively working together in a very focused and successful way.

It was important to have a range of 'on the shelf' articles and information sheets about the guide. The Development Worker was able to use these directly, for example by circulating via e-mail to local authority staff and indirectly by providing background information to the public relations workers.

Finally, changing the strategy to offering a guide directly to families shows that a flexible approach needs to be adopted at all times so that contingency plans can easily be put in place.

Multidisciplinary workshops

The local and national studies previously referred to in **Chapter two** and the parents' focus group all agree that professionals such as nurses, doctors, social workers and teachers working on a daily basis with families are very important sources of information to families. Taking this into account, a series of six free workshops were organised by the

Development Worker of Newcastle Special Needs Network (NSNN) in February and March 2001. The NSNN Development Worker was also a member of the steering group for the guide and this enabled a seamless link between the theory, planning and practice.

The aims of the workshops were to:

- launch and introduce the guide to workers;
- maximise on the workers' professional relationships with families to publicise the guide to parents;
- provide workers with a practical tool in their information giving roles;
- provide an opportunity for workers to network with others from different organisations working with disabled children and their families;
- foster and share ideas about providing reliable and timely information to families.

There was a very good response to the advertising of the free workshops and 122 places were booked. The Development Worker from NSNN and parents acted as facilitators for the workshops. Other parents contributed and shared their thoughts and ideas throughout some of the sessions.

During the workshops, the workers discussed how they would publicise the guide to parents and the following box lists the different ways that they identified.

How workers can promote the guide to users

- Hang the guide on a notice board
- Have leaflets handy
- Have 'inspection' copies
- Visit parents and promote the guide
- Have a sample copy in the library
- Take a guide to events
- Emphasise the guide is 'free'
- Share the guide with parents and young people
- Use in parenting classes.

Each participant was asked to complete an evaluation form at the end of their session and out of the 73 people who did so, 46 people had found the workshop 'very useful', and 26 'useful' and one 'not very useful'.

Some of the reasons for finding the workshops useful are summarised here and reflect workers' awareness and willingness to address many of the issues raised in **Chapter two**, for example, that services can be fragmented between different organisations:

- Being able to understand disability from other professionals' perspective or from the parent's perspective.
- Getting a wider view of the process through which a family passes "before I see them".
- Prevents 'tunnel vision' and promotes appreciation for other roles within the family's environment (education, and so on) and also, most importantly, what the family needs and wants.

Most respondents felt that all aspects of the workshop had been useful, however, some would have liked more time, while one or two thought the sessions were too long. Some individuals found the following the least useful:

- finding out about problems facing other professionals;
- session called 'what information do parents need and where do they get it'.

This feedback indicates that for some workers the two issues of general information provision and gaining a better understanding of other organisations roles do not seem to be a priority. This may be due to the 'heavy workloads' of workers, as previously identified by parents. Gaining a better understanding of what is happening here may be a focus for further work.

Finally, the evaluation forms provided many comments and suggestions that indicate the workshops had been one way of enhancing awareness about information provision and a good opportunity for workers to see services to families in a more multi-agency context.

At the end of the series of workshops the NSNN Development Worker concluded:

> The workshops proved to be an excellent opportunity for interagency working and extensive information exchange ... there were a number of issues raised around information and the impact of having (and not having it) on the lives of disabled children.

three

The follow up from the workshops with questionnaires and individual interviews

The steering group and NSNN felt that it was important to find out from workers 'what had happened in the following months'; for example, had workers been able to publicise the guide, did they have feedback from parents about its usefulness, did they find it useful themselves? **Chapters four** and **five** describe the feedback and research work.

Working in partnership

In one respect, the development of a guide to services in Newcastle upon Tyne can be viewed as a positive example of some of the traditional 'working together' skills that can be found in statutory and voluntary organisations. A wide range of people came together determined to make the project work. Many partnerships were formed and the relationship that developed with the Patient Information Centre (PIC) demonstrates very clearly the value of this way of working.

The PIC was the 'contact' organisation for parents and workers wishing to obtain a copy of the guide. The PIC has a wide range of health and social care information for members of the public and professionals. The service is funded by the NHS, is free and confidential and is available each weekday. The PIC is based in the Newcastle General Hospital site in the west of the city, where there are extensive information resources including

access to the NHS Direct database of local and *national* services. One of the attractions of working in partnership with the PIC was their ability to offer a comprehensive information service to parents to complement the signposting information in the guide.

Over a period of months, a very close and positive working relationship developed and many aspects of the whole project were discussed and explored during regular meetings between the PIC manager and the Development Worker. This ongoing and effective communication enabled procedures to be in place prior to the production of the guide and speedy agreement on further strategies as required.

Members of the PIC team attended the workshops to familiarise themselves with the guide and to help other agencies understand how families could get their own copy.

Contributions of the Patient Information Centre

- Sending out copies of the guide as a result of requests from parents and workers via telephone calls, Typetalk and Textphone, e-mails, people calling into the centre and an answering machine (for out of hour's calls).
- Assisting with developing the publicity strategy and providing practical tools; for example, mailing lists of health visitors and of services available in Newcastle upon Tyne for people from black and ethnic minority groups.

- Directly publicising the guide in their newsletter (distribution list of over 1,000 including statutory and voluntary organisations), via the NHS e-mail and through their extensive networking system.
- Distributing sample copies of the guide and publicity materials; for example, sample guides and posters were sent to local doctors.
- Acting as a contact point for people requesting further supplies of publicity materials.
- Providing the Development Worker with monitoring information using their 'caller log' sheet.
- Advising on and agreeing procedures for dealing with callers outside Newcastle upon Tyne local authority area, complaints or concerns about the guide and requests for multiple copies.
- Receiving and forwarding to the Development Worker the 'What do you think of your guide' feedback forms inserted in the guide.
- Listening to parents and workers comments when calling for a guide and identified themes; for example, some parents seemed to need 'permission' from a worker before feeling confident to ask for a guide.

Between February and August 2001 the Development Worker distributed 1,088 guides as well as 3,000 leaflets and 445 posters to professionals and community groups. The numbers include sample copies of the guide for professionals' own use and supplies of guides for targeted groups of professionals, for example, the Children's Community Nursing Team to offer directly to families.

During the same period the PIC distributed 1,068 guides, 7,000 leaflets and 555 posters. The numbers of guides include 682 guides distributed to professionals and 378 individual requests.

In the absence of accurate statistics concerning the numbers and circumstances of disabled children in Newcastle upon Tyne, the steering group had made an 'informed guess' regarding the amount of guides that would be needed. Faced with this uncertainty it was important for the Development Worker to set up a system to keep track of the numbers distributed. Within seven months approximately 2,200 had been distributed, indicating that the original figure of 3,000 printed was a reasonable 'guess'.

The PIC provided the Development Worker with monitoring information about the 378 individual requests for a guide between February and August 2001 and the following graphs give some helpful information about the:

- gender of callers;
- type of caller;
- area requests originate;
- method of contact;
- publicity source of requests.

Some comparisons have been made with statistics for the same period of time of people contacting the PIC for other types of information (ie, not for a guide). Although these comparisons are very basic, it may be that further research or work could help inform information strategies.

three

Chart one: gender

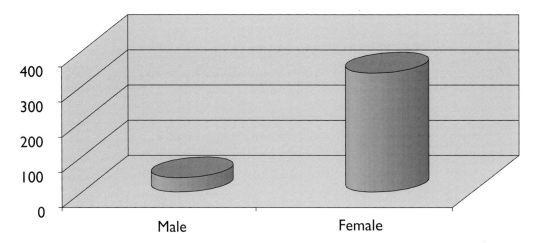

It is typical for more females to contact information services like the PIC and the distribution of 'guide' callers between male and female similarly reflects this trend. This raises issues concerning 'who' the traditional carers of disabled children are.

Chart two: caller type

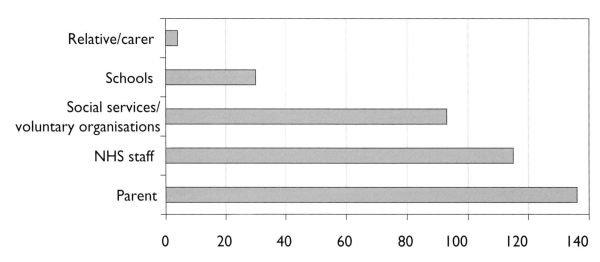

Thirty per cent of routine contacts ('non-guide' requests) with the PIC were NHS staff, compared to a larger number of over 50% of the 'guide contacts' that were NHS staff. There were similar patterns noted for contacts from people in other organisations, for example, social services and the voluntary sector. Further data will be needed to understand these trends.

Chart three: area

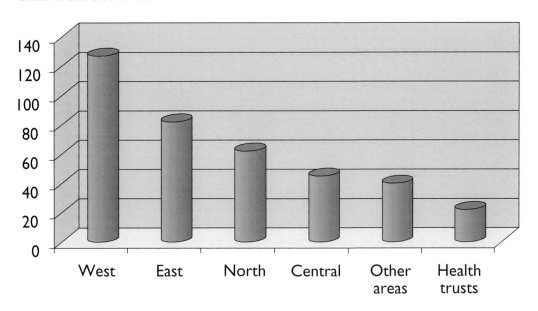

The statistics show the largest numbers of callers are from the west part of the city. This information has been included for interest, as there needs to be further work to understand its meaning.

Chart four: contact method

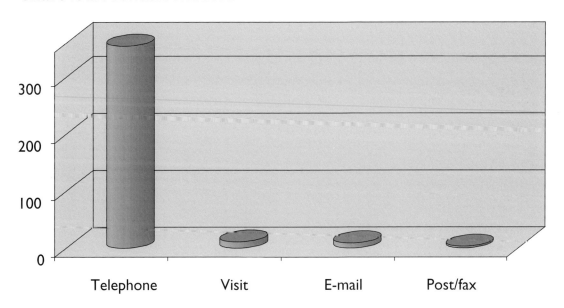

From this evidence, the main medium for requesting a guide was the telephone. Over 90% of people requesting a guide did so via the telephone compared to a much lower figure of 26% of people using the telephone to request other types of information from the PIC. Even workers who knew about the guide from e-mail publicity used the telephone, although this may reflect the wording of the publicity itself.

three

Chart five: publicity

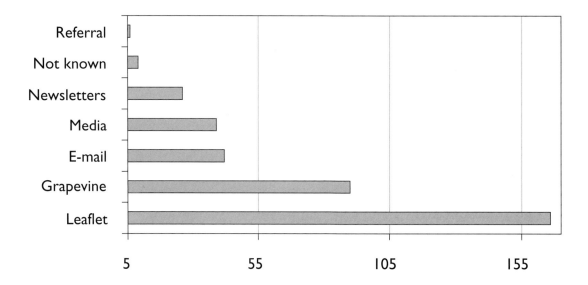

Popular opinion suggests 'word of mouth' is a very significant information strategy. However, this data shows that posters and leaflets were the most commonly quoted publicity source followed by 'word of mouth'. Of those requesting a guide via posters and leaflets: 34% were parents, 17% NHS staff, 35% agencies such as social services, and 14% were schools/students. It was surprising that the more direct method of three different free papers delivered to each household elicited so few requests. When Newcastle has a robust register of disabled children, it will be interesting to compare this response to a direct mailing of a 'leaflet' to patients' homes.

'Referral' was the least quoted publicity source. In this context 'referral' is the suggestion/recommendation from a professional that a parent obtains a guide. This was disappointing given that many professionals were aware of the guide. The research and evaluation phase of the work covered in **Chapters four** and **five** describe workers general perceptions of information, their role as information providers and more specifically, their views and usage of the guide to services for parents.

Understanding the use of the guide in family contexts

This chapter and **Chapter five** present the findings of research carried out after the launch of the guide (see **Appendix B** for details of the research methodology). The guide was launched in February 2001, and the post-launch research was carried out between April 2001 and June 2001. This chapter looks at parents' perceptions of information and the guide.

General comments about the guide

Parents see the guide as a 'good first step' in the development of information for carers of disabled children. Generally parents (and professionals) recognise that the guide's function is a 'signposting' one that enables parents and professionals to identify relevant services to meet particular needs. Parents who have several years' experience of bringing up disabled children (in this report such parents will be referred to as 'experienced parents') feel that the guide is useful and they wish they had had one when their disabled child was young. These parents think that the guide is useful for a person at the start of the 'learning curve' of being a parent of a disabled child as well as offering new information for experienced parents.

Most parents in the post-launch focus group think that the guide is useful as it specialises in the needs of parents with disabled children. They think that the presentation and layout of the guide is good. Parents say it is easy to read and is clear. Some parents comment that perhaps the sections of the guide could be made more visible by either having coloured cards or tabbed section headings. Parents raise the issue of information remaining current and suggest that the guide could be put on a website "so that the information can be updated easily and promptly". Parents think that the main problem for navigating the guide is that parents really need to know the condition of their child and have an 'identifiable problem' to get the most out of the guide. The early stages of recognising that a child has a form of disability often entails just having a 'collection of symptoms' rather than a diagnosis, which makes the guide less useful in these types of contexts. Nonetheless the guide still has the potential to help parents in the early stages of identifying a condition by signposting them to relevant professionals to help obtain a diagnosis. One parent's story summarises many of these issues:

> "My daughter has dyspraxia. We fought for a long time to get this recognised. It was a hard, hard struggle to get doctors to assess her. She is 14 now and we have only just got it on her statement that she is dyspraxic. I got to know who to approach from Newcastle Special

Needs Network (NSNN). Mandy told me where to go. A friend knew someone who had symptoms exactly like [daughter] and so she has had a look at the guide and she is now contacting Social Services etc. It is much easier to get help if you have a name for your child's condition and she is using the guide to start this process. One problem with it is that you need to know who to go through to access the services in the guide. A parent's referral is not always possible. You might have to go through a GP or Social Worker.

The services behind the information

All parents welcome the guide as a source of information, as it helps them to obtain the services they need. However, they raise five main issues about access to services:

1) Services do not have enough resources to meet demand, which often results in long waiting lists. Therefore, parents often have to wait before they access a service; a parent quotes the occupational therapy service as one example.
2) Gaining access to services can involve complicated referral processes, which makes access to services a complex and lengthy process.
3) Some parents say that they experience problems in getting their child's condition 'statemented'. Parents often notice symptoms in their children that warrant concern and they have to push for further exploration before

instigating the process of getting a child 'statemented'.
4) Parents feel that some schools are not sympathetic to the needs of disabled children and do not recognise their special needs.
5) Parents say formal networks such as NSNN and their own informal networks are very valuable resources for them.

Parents and the guide

A difficulty that many parents' face is getting their child's disability recognised. One parent says "it was a hard, hard struggle to get doctors to assess [my daughter]". Many parents argue that it "was easier to get help if you have a name for your child's condition". The experienced parents feel that the guide can help with this particular difficulty as it will help parents know who to go through to gain access to services and therefore help identify a particular 'condition'. This issue of having access to services based on the labelling of a child's condition seems to be the most problematic for understanding the role and use of the guide for parents/ carers of disabled children. Nonetheless, response to the guide is good, as the following comments show.

Direct feedback from the '*What do you think of your guide?*' forms provide some insights into what parents and professionals think of the guide, and they show that parents and workers find the guide easy to use and useful. The guide is also useful in raising awareness of the services that are available in Newcastle upon Tyne.

The following is information collated from the 21 feedback forms and it also includes a selection of the comments made by parents to some open-ended questions.

How easy do you find the guide to use?

	Parents	Workers	Unknown
Very easy	8	9	I
Easy	2	I	0
Very difficult	0	0	0
Total	**I0**	**I0**	**I**

How easy do you find the contents and index to use?

	Parents	Workers	Unknown
Very easy	8	8	I
Easy	2	2	0
Very difficult	0	0	0
Total	**I0**	**I0**	**I**

How useful do you find the guide?

	Parents	Workers	Unknown
Very useful	6	6	I
Useful	3	3	0
Slightly useful	0	0	0
Total	**9**	**9**	**I**

Two people did not respond to the question.

Does the guide increase your awareness of services in Newcastle upon Tyne?

	Parents	Workers	Unknown
Greatly increased	6	3	0
Increased	3	6	0
Slightly increased	I	I	0
Total	**I0**	**I0**	**0**

One person did not respond to the question.

four

Parents' comments show that the guide meets some of the needs of carers and has consequently been well received. It is clear that many carers struggle to understand any systems of support and very often are not aware of what services are available to them, for example, carers say:

"I wish that a document like this had been around 5 years ago when it became apparent that my son, now 7, had a speech and developmental problem. I initially found the whole 'system' regarding 'special needs' to be a complete minefield at a time when I was an emotional wreck; if only this information had been available then, it would have made my life so much easier."

"Parents/carers need a lot more help and information. If they do not see social workers etc, they wouldn't find out any information at all ... it has taken 14 years for myself to find out there is a great deal of help out there."

"The information provided alongside each section and organisation is extremely helpful. It gives you an idea of who does what and also helps you to find other organisations and facilities that you may not have known about."

Carers find the guide easy to use and comment that it is "easy to handle, format good, clear print, well thought out, good overall". They find the sections of the guide that relate to health, social services and other services helpful, with carers saying that the "the various sections were extremely helpful – it is much easier, all the information being in the one book. Sometimes you are unsure as to where to look for information and this guide has made it very easy". Another parent said that s/he "found all the sections very useful, all I needed to know about different things to do with having a disabled son". Carers also felt that the guide gave enough information about each organisation and commented that very basic information such as opening hours and details of how to contact services is very useful. They say, for example, that "there is more than adequate information for each organisation, and yet not too much, which can sometimes leave you dreading having to look for a service or information. A well-thought-through document with services that I did not know existed". Another parent comments: "yes, very useful about all the things like opening hours and other things about the services".

All of these comments show that generally there is a lack of relevant information in an appropriate form to enable carers to manage the care of disabled children. One carer for example says that the guide is "very helpful. My daughter is 14 years old and this is the *first time* I have ever been given anything with this information".

Some themes identified by the Patient Information Centre

In addition to themes that emerge out of the research with parents, the information team at the PIC identify a number of themes from the many verbal comments they receive from parents who call to ask for a guide. The themes are:

- Many of the parent callers seem to think that they need 'permission' from, for example, a doctor or nurse before ringing for a guide. Parents do not see it as something that they are empowered to do without this 'permission'.
- Occasionally parents are not sure exactly what they are ringing for and they say that their teacher or nurse, etc, has told them to ring.
- Parents feel the need to clarify that the guide is 'free' – there is an expectation by some that they would have to pay for the guide (this sometimes happens when callers ring public sector information providers).
- Generally parents are extremely 'pleased' that the information is available – 'if only this had been around before' is a common response.
- Some GPs suggest that parents ring for the guide and this is viewed as very positive by the information staff as it is not common for GPs to recommend 'named information'.

These comments and the information from the feedback forms support what many of the parents say in the focus group research. Parents want information to be easily accessible and clearly presented. When they are in the situation of caring for a disabled child they want to be aware of what services are available to help them manage the situation. They see the signposting guide as a useful tool to help them achieve a reasonable quality of life both for their child and for the family unit as a whole.

Parents' perceptions of information

Parents value having information – they say that having access to services through information makes them feel more in charge of their child's care. They feel that information increases their power as it helps them to fight what they perceive as 'barriers' to getting services for their children. They say the guide is very useful because it gives them information about where to access further information. Awareness of what information and services are available is varied among the parents in the focus groups. Some parents are well informed about services and about the medical and social aspects of their child's condition as well as what rights and benefits they are entitled to. On the other hand, some parents are amazed at the amount of information and range of services listed in the guide.

four

Parents' thoughts about key working issues

Although the research did not focus specifically on key working, parents did raise the key working issue in relation to gaining access to and using information (for details of key working see Mukherjee et al, 1999). There are several points that relate to key working and information. First many parents feel that professionals are not enabled to distribute information, often citing that professionals might choose not to pass on information because of their heavy workloads. Also parents' state that their main information need is details of benefits and comment that not all professionals have a clear and detailed knowledge of benefits. Generally they think that professionals should give more information, particularly those based in hospitals and schools. They point out that there are many key stages in a disabled child's biography as well as general ongoing concerns that require information to configure support at a particular transition or to sustain support over a period of time. This is where parents feel that a key worker in relation to and combined with information would be helpful. A key worker would provide support for parents accessing and using the information and would also help them to coordinate the many services the children require due to their complex needs. As one parent explains:

"I think having a guide is a good idea, but there are still too many people to go to. You still have to go from one professional to another. A key worker would be a good idea. My daughter has Turner's Syndrome and I knew before the professionals just by talking to a friend who had a child with similar symptoms. I think hospitals should explain about benefits. Many people are missing out on these benefits but the professionals should be the information providers. You often find out about these benefits through friends."

In relation to confidentiality many parents are not concerned that details about their child would be shared between agencies if 'key working' practices were established. They feel that many professionals work on a 'need to know' basis that acts as a constraint in coordinating services. As one parent says, "I think professionals get hung up on this 'need to know' thing". Often a parent does not mind who knows as long as they are getting the correct support. Some parents feel that professionals can use the issue of confidentiality as an excuse for inaction.

Parents are generally concerned that information both for themselves and between professionals is not being shared as well as it could be. Several reasons are cited; in particular, practical issues such as overwork and ethical issues such as confidentiality. Parents want to have more information and they want information to be shared between professionals to ensure that their child gets the support s/he needs.

Other issues about information for parents

Parents raise a number of interesting points that are useful in considering the development of information and other services. They feel that it might be useful to have a register of children with disabilities so that mailings could be sent straight to parents. Some parents think that even if any mailings arrived at the 'wrong time' for parents, they could just 'put the information away' until it is needed. At least parents would be aware that the information is available.

Another aspect of providing information relates to 'consultation' or 'participation' processes. Parents think that the more information they have, the more they want to feed into services. Parents say that they could then help to 'shape the services', but they think that this means establishing a new process that would need additional resources.

Among parents there is concern about waiting lists. Many parents think that, however much they are consulted, unless there are sufficient resources to fund services, changes in services will not materialise to meet the needs of parents and children.

Parents suggest that schools should have a 'fieldworker' for channelling information from other services and parents into the school and vice versa. One example parents give is the case of giving "health information to school say, from a community paediatrician". At a more specific level, and although parents recognise that it is important to rise above anecdote, most parents state that the education department is reluctant to provide statements of educational need.

Many parents experience even more difficulties if their child 'does not fit into a convenient slot'. They think that this is where multi-agency working and the provision of information are very important, as both enable services to be delivered according to the complex needs of the child rather than satisfying the categories of the service providers. Parents feel that information would help them to understand their child's condition and help them to get the support that they and their children need. There is a consensus that parents want their children to be able to live fulfilled independent lives in the community, and therefore services and information need to be available to meet the specific support needs of their children.

Parents express concern about the ways in which services do or do not work together and they state that it would help them if service providers coordinated their work to provide a more cohesive service that is easier to navigate. They feel that joining up services and cross-referencing between services are both very important in providing a service that would meet the needs of a child and a family unit. At the moment parents have to work out the relationships between services, including coordinating appointments, information and advice by themselves.

four

Summary and analysis of research with parents

The research carried out in Newcastle upon Tyne supports the findings of many other studies about the experiences of parents of disabled children.

Parents feel that they need information so that they can overcome the 'barriers' to getting services for their children. Parents' think that individual workers do not always give appropriate or comprehensive information to them in their own given situation. They feel that due to the complex nature of child disability generally, they would benefit from some sort of key working arrangement to coordinate services for disabled children. They are concerned about the ways in which agencies are not coordinating services; they feel that they want agencies to work together and share information so that children's needs are met. They are also concerned about the lack of resources that are available for services, and fear that this will lead to further waiting lists for services.

There is considerable ambiguity about the processes of having a child's condition recognised, having a child 'statemented', achieving 'diagnosis', and just referral processes in general. Many parents say that 'you learn about those processes, as you become more experienced'. This point relates to the issue of information, and the guide highlights an area of unmet information need as it is not designed to meet the specific needs of parents who are at the pre-diagnosis stage of child disability. However, parents think that the guide can still be helpful in the pre-diagnosis stage because it can help parents to find out whom to go to for help in the process of getting a child's condition recognised. Apart from this point, the guide is seen as an excellent tool for parents because it will help to raise their awareness of services and help them access local community services. To sum up, many parents do welcome the guide, they like the design of the guide, find it easy to use, and see it as a useful tool to help them care for their children.

Understanding the use of the guide in service contexts

The research also sought to understand perceptions about the guide and the provision of information of a variety of professionals working with children with disabilities. To understand the ways in which information is being used by the variety of professionals involved in multi-agency work, the researchers asked them to outline their roles and responsibilities and then discuss information and the guide within the dynamics of roles and responsibilities. This is particularly pertinent as all the workers are developing multi-agency services where their roles are in the process of being redefined. This chapter outlines and discusses the perspectives and experiences of those professionals involved in the care of disabled children who are starting to work in a 'joined up' way. The qualitative interviews and the open-ended postal survey show that professionals form a network around the care needs of a child and family. The actual nature of these networks needs further exploration but nonetheless they are an important part of a 'care strategy'. Further sources of data are the 'What do you think of your guide?' feedback forms and direct feedback to the Development Worker, which are also included in **Appendix A**.

General comments about the guide

Professionals view the guide as a 'good first step' in the development of information for carers of disabled children, and recognise that it acts as a 'signpost' to identify relevant services to meet particular needs. Professionals use the guide in a variety of ways in relation to their roles and responsibilities in the care of children with disabilities. They all think that the guide is an important part of the broader provision of service for children with disabilities. These general comments suggest that the guide needs to be understood by considering the ways in which parents perceive and interpret information within the dynamics of the provision of services, which includes professional practice.

five

Planning and Development Officer, Carers Information Officer, Information Manager

General roles and responsibilities, perceptions of information

This group of professionals' perspective focuses on the publicising and distribution of information for service users and for service planning and development processes. The Information Manager works for NHS Health Trusts, the Carers Information Officer works for Newcastle Council for Voluntary Service (Newcastle Carers Project). The Planning and Development Officer works for the Local Education Authority (LEA) and is involved with the Childcare and Early Years Education Provider. They are all in contact with a range of statutory and voluntary sector organisations.

The roles and responsibilities of the information professionals include:

- The delivery of health information directly to the public and to health professionals. This involves the actual delivery of an information service for carers, for (external) professionals and for (internal) staff, including a telephone helpline, library, in-house publications, and in the near future an information point in the centre of Newcastle.
- The planning post involves encouraging new provision and supporting existing provision.

The nature of their contact with families varies. Members of the public usually access the Carers Information Officer via the carers' helpline service. Sometimes they contact the service via e-mail, fax and the traditional postal service. The planning and development professional does not have any direct contact with children or individual providers. The frequency of contact the information providers have with service users is difficult to assess. One of the professionals estimates that s/he has contact with parent carers/families approximately six times a month. They state that they need information about who to pass on information to, as well as information on a variety of information sources and tools. They think the guide is "an excellent, quick reference information tool and we keep a copy to hand at all times". The planning professional says that s/he needs a range of information about specific conditions and sources of help and support.

The professionals use the following sources of information: various databases, books, leaflets and the Internet. Other sources are a variety of organisations, libraries and colleagues. Further sources are their own information resource including staff, the Patient Information Centre, NHS Direct, Disability North, Social Services information and Newcastle Council for Voluntary Service (information resource and staff). Further sets of sources are the Newcastle Health and Social Care Directory, the guide and a selection of other tools such as the 'advice finder' on a personal computer.

The professionals say that parents need simple straightforward advice about what they are entitled to. This includes knowing who can offer help and support and how to access agencies and what the agencies do and do not do. Parents also need information about how others cope and where to find peer support.

One professional says that her own research shows that parents have wide and varying information needs, but what is most important is how parents get information as well as how good it is, and when and why they get it. She argues that everything points to parents/carers wanting a single human contact for all their information needs, plus flexible access to electronic and hard copy information sources. Therefore, she feels that it is important to offer a single-entry access point to a single system or directory guide to parents.

Use of the guide

The workers have seen the guide and they found out about it from mail shots, professional networks and from the launch workshop. They have supplies of guides from NSNN and from the Development Worker to distribute to parents. They promote the guide by including articles in newsletters and sending out flyers. They put items about the guide in the *WEB* (a newsletter for professionals working with carers and interested in carers' issues) and send flyers to WINE (Workers in Information North East). They also promote the guide through word of mouth recommendation and e-mail. They send direct mail adverts to members of the Early Years Development and Childcare Partnership (EYDCP), and the guide is available from the Children's Information Service (CIS).

The professionals do not know how many other people have the guide, but they comment that many members of the health staff seem to have it. One of the information workers handed out 12 copies, and the planning officer knows three people who have the guide. They think that the guide is well advertised. They feel that sometimes professionals do not think that some of the new information is relevant to them due to the 'information overload' that professionals face. They feel that parents can get the guide easily; however, in their experience they find that parents are sometimes reluctant to telephone for a copy unless they have been 'given permission' from a health professional. They also say that some parents are concerned about cost, even though the guide is free.

These professionals say that feedback from parents about the guide is very positive, and parents' comments include "I wish I'd had this years ago" and "I've been looking for something like this". The professionals feel the guide is useful in pointing parents in the right direction for the services they need and helps to raise awareness of what is on offer generally and where to go for help.

The professionals think that the information in the guide is well presented. It follows the 'accessible information guidelines' and is therefore easy to read and use and 'about the right size'. They feel that the guide provides information parents might need and that it contains information that they and other professionals might not know about. One information worker says that the guide

five

"seems to bring all the important basic information and contacts together to enable people to manage their own information seeking if they should wish to do so".

One professional says that their own research shows that, on the whole, carers prefer to manage their own information seeking. S/he comments that carers "just want the tools and skills to achieve this". In relation to this point s/he feels that the guide is an "excellent tool to support this" aspiration. Some of the professionals use the guide in their everyday work, but they say that the guide is still at the stage of early use.

In general terms, these workers see information as an essential part of service delivery, especially given the fact that one service alone cannot meet the needs of a particular family, therefore information about services is needed so that workers and carers can construct a package of support. The planning officer thinks that it was a very good idea to use a workshop to launch the guide because it not only helped to raise awareness of the guide, but it also helped to educate workers in how to use information for carers and in the workers' own practices.

Specialist School Health Nurses (SSHNs)

General roles and responsibilities, perceptions of information

All the SSHNs who responded to the survey are in contact with other agencies. Their contacts include members of staff who are employed by the Primary Care NHS Trust, Prudhoe and Northgate NHS Trust and the Mental Health NHS Trust.

In general terms they describe their responsibility as:

- planning individual nursing care for children with complex needs within schools and in the home environment at citywide level;
- advising, supporting and training children, families and educational staff.

The nature of their contact with families of disabled children reflects this and includes school and home visits, attending hospital appointments with the family and providing advocacy. The frequency of contact is determined on the basis of the needs of the child and the family and can vary from once a day in some cases to once a school term in other cases.

The type of information they need is that which will support children and families in maintaining a good quality of life. They also need a history of the child's condition via nursing assessments and they need to know which other agencies are involved in the care of the child. There also needs to be some identification of the concerns and needs of the child and family. The SSHNs report that they get their information from other multidisciplinary personnel, their own past experience, various courses and training, articles/journals/pamphlets, health promotion activities and the Newcastle Health and Social Care Directory. Other sources of information include the Internet, libraries and 'Yellow Pages'. SSHNs cite various professionals such as physiotherapists, educational staff and social workers as other sources of information. Charities are also information sources.

The SSHNs see the role of information in the delivery of services as: 1) central in developing and conducting evidence-based practice; and 2) a pivotal component in the access aspect of service delivery, as parents need to be aware of what services are available to them and know how to access them. The SSHNs say that parents need information about their child's condition, support groups and who to contact about specific issues. This also involves information about how to contact particular services and groups and what to ask. In general the SSHNs say that parents need information about what services and resources are available.

Use of the guide

All the SSHNs have seen the guide. They found out about the guide via posters and through the training day held by NSNN as well as from other professionals. At the time of the guide's launch the nurses obtained the guide in a variety of ways, which included being given a copy by their team leader, getting copies through the post, and getting copies at the guide training day and launch.

In general, the SSHNs promote the guide by personal recommendations to parents and by distributing leaflets, as well as by general word of mouth. Nurses also give the guide to educational staff.

In relation to general issues of the availability of the guide, all the members of the nursing team have a copy of the guide. They comment that the guide is easy to obtain for professionals. The nurses have mixed perceptions of the ease of availability of the guide for parents: some think that parents can obtain it easily, while others think that it might be difficult to obtain. Some nurses comment that parents are reluctant to 'apply' for the guide; however, they do not offer a reason why this is the case. Nurses give copies to parents and the only feedback they have from parents is that the guide is 'useful'.

The SSHNs think that the guide is easy to use and self-explanatory with lots of relevant information. In relation to the design, they think the guide is attractive and easy to recognise and as one nurse says "easy to find in a pile". They comment that the large print is good in that it makes the guide easy to read and they also say that the instructions are clear about how to use the guide.

Some SSHNs use the guide with parents and others do not. Those who have not used it comment that they have not yet had a situation in which they feel they have needed it. The SSHNs who use it in their work say that they find it very useful as it helps them to provide parents with relevant up-to-date information on a variety of issues. One SSHN says that she finds the guide very helpful in relation to

five

housing issues and for how to apply for grants to help with building work. Another SSHN says that she gives the guide to parents and shows them how to find their own information. Some of the nurses have 'used [the guide] several times' and other nurses have used the guide 'four times plus professional use'. In general terms, the SSHNs think that the guide does provide the sort of information that service users need. The nurses also find that the guide provides them with information that they did not know about. They think that it is "excellent", "useful and wide ranging" and "user friendly".

One area of concern the SSHNs have is that special schools are not identified in the education section and that SSHNs should be identified in the introduction of the health section. One SSHN also suggests that SSHNs, social workers and community nurses should all be on one list as 'The Children with Disabilities Team'. Generally, the nurses see information as very necessary in the delivery of services and that information needs to be easily accessible and easy to understand.

Children's Community Nurses (CCNs)

General roles and responsibilities, perceptions of information

The CCNs of the Newcastle Hospitals NHS Trust (who responded to our survey) work with other service providers. The CCNs say they work with staff of the Primary Care NHS Trust, Prudhoe and Northgate NHS Trust, the Mental Health NHS Trust and with staff working for social services.

Their roles and responsibilities include:

- providing nursing care for children with complex health needs;
- training and supporting carers;
- the provision of technical care and support;
- coordinating service delivery;
- the revision and development of clinical protocols.

One nurse sees their contact with families as a 'generalist' nurse in the community, who liaises closely with specialist services, facilitates discharges from hospitals and seeks to prevent admissions to hospital. Nurses' tasks include conducting home visits and doing assessments. They provide ongoing support, coordinate care and liaise with the care team. The community liaison nurse provides language support for families whose preferred language is not English. General health promotion is also one of their responsibilities.

Nurses state that the frequency of contact with families varies, with intervention depending on need. Contact may be daily in some cases, or weekly in other cases, with some less often than that. Nurses say that often contacts are made "when necessary and when able to fit it in with current caseloads … more often than not in a crisis", which suggests that CCNs are struggling to meet the demands for the service.

The CCNs say that they need good community knowledge of local facilities and services for families and children with disabilities. They need good networks with other professionals and agencies, access to libraries, IT, specialist subject information sources, and access to information about services at both local and national level. Their usual sources of information are members of nursing and medical staff, parents and carers as well as libraries, the Internet, specialist departments and academic courses. Other sources are circulars, the guide, Contact a Family and their own knowledge. Word of mouth is mentioned, as is health promotion material. The nurses identify one gap, which is the lack of available information leaflets in ethnic minority languages.

The CCNs think that parents need accurate information that is specific to their child, as and when they need it, and in a form that parents can understand. Parents also need information about services and how to access them and they need information about benefits. One

nurse says that often a one-to-one session with written information works well with families to help them understand what is relevant to them. Not all families, however, have English as their first language, so information must be available in different languages. Nurses say that information on video about a child's condition is useful. They also say that parents need information about any diagnosis that is made as well as any treatments and facilities that may be available in relation to their child's condition.

In general terms, information and giving information is an integral part of the CCNs' work. They see information as a way to help parents know how to care for their child and ensure the child's health and well-being. Parents need information about their child's condition, how to access support services, how to obtain benefits and contact self-help groups. Information also plays a part in cases of advocacy, in the practical tasks of filling in forms and in applying for funds such as the Family Fund. Information is central to preventive aspects of community services as seen, for instance, in health promotion activities. Information about disabilities is seen as important, especially information that conveys the meaning of the disability both for the child and the family in their everyday lives, as well as knowing how to plan for the future.

five

Use of the guide

All the CCNs who responded to the survey have seen the guide. They became aware of the guide through personal and professional networks. They obtain copies of it from the Patient Information Centre and from their place of work.

The CCNs promote the guide through word of mouth, by making recommendations to health visitors and other professionals as well as to families. The CCNs circulate leaflets about the guide and also distribute copies to carers and other agencies.

All these professionals have the guide and say that all the members of their teams and associated teams have copies too. They feel that access to the guide is easy for both parents and professionals. They have not had any feedback from parents about the guide.

They see the role of the guide as useful in raising awareness of the range of services that are available for families, so enabling families to make their own choices about which services they would like to access. The nurses think the guide is easy to read and to use. They say that the format is "useful", and the design is "nice" and it "looks interesting".

The CCNs think that the guide provides the type of information that parents need. The nurses say that it provides them with information that they did not know. Some CCNs use the guide with parents and others do not. Initial use of the guide by the CCNs both for themselves and with parents varied from between ten and twenty times to two and three times in the time between the guide's launch in February 2001 and the time of the survey in April–June 2001.

In relation to making improvements to the guide, the CCNs raise the issue of keeping the information current. They feel that more information is needed about individual services and that information about 'very local support' would be helpful, for example, support in the West End of Newcastle like 'Families First', 'Baby Sitting Service', and the 'Toy Library for Children with Special Needs'. The nurses also feel that leaflets and videos should be available in ethnic minority languages and that any audio tapes should be easily accessible from one place. They note that the Special Needs Schools Nursing Service is not mentioned in the introduction to the health section, and they feel that it would be appropriate to do so as it would establish a different client group to the mainstream schools nurses.

As shown, information and the giving of information is an integral part of the service that the CCNs provide. It helps them to ensure the well-being of a child by helping the parents to understand the meaning of the child's disability and for parents to be aware of support services.

Social workers and family support workers

General roles and responsibilities, perceptions of information

This category includes a paediatric hospital-based social worker, a social worker in the community and a family support worker in the voluntary sector (Barnardo's).

They all work with other agencies that provide services for children in Newcastle upon Tyne, including the Hospital Trust, social services and charities in the area. They work with health professionals, SENTASS, educational psychologists, physiotherapists and CCNs. Roles and responsibilities vary:

- The hospital-based social worker role involves assessment of needs and supporting families with children in hospital with head injuries, neurology and other non-specialised illnesses.
- The roles of the social workers in the community are strategic planning, quality issues and budget management as well as line management responsibilities.
- The family support workers manage nurseries and work with families who need extra support: this ranges from 'having someone to talk to', to practical help and directing families to appropriate services.

The nature of contact with families for community social workers involves consultation, dealing with complaints and strategic planning. Generally, their contact with families is weekly for consultation and/or complaints. The paediatric social worker's contact with the child and family is mainly hospital based, but with some home visits. It involves assessments and includes some child protection issues. They are often in contact with children in hospital on a daily basis when the child is in crisis. Thereafter, there is variable contact at clinics or in types of more active follow-up work. Typically, contact with children and families who are not in hospital is once a fortnight. The family support worker's contact with children and families centres around their inclusion policy, which means that parents/carers of disabled children can request a nursery place provided the child is two years old or over and lives in their 'catchment' area. Contact is mainly through children attending the nursery, although anyone living in the area can potentially call in for support, information and advice.

The community social workers need information about the number and circumstances of children with disabilities and what services are available. They need information about the quality and usage of services, as well as any gaps in service provision. They also want information on local and central government priorities and initiatives.

Paediatric social workers need information about support groups and information about charitable trusts and how to access them. They also need information about welfare rights advice and in this context there are two main issues:

1) Many parents are employed and have problems staying with children in hospital.

2) There are complex linkages between low-paid work and benefits on which parents need advice.

Team leaders of family support work say that they need 'information on information'; for instance, they would like to have more detailed information so that they can back up the information in the guide. They also need information about school nursery places available to children with disabilities and special needs.

The paediatric social worker thinks that parents need information about health, namely what is happening to their child. Parents need information about finance, for example, how to manage being away from home and work while the child is in hospital (parents staying in hospital with their child can be as far as 50 to 100 miles away from home). Parents also need information about accommodation while staying at the hospital and about support and services, especially in relation to the move from hospital to back home. Furthermore, parents generally need advice about 'how to find information'. Social workers think that parents need specialist information about the needs of their child and general information about the range of services available and how to access them.

Usual sources of information for paediatric social workers include the welfare rights 'phone line', colleagues and managers. They also get information about rare conditions and medicine from the Internet and the library. Social workers say they obtain information from parents and other professionals. They also get their information from management systems, reports and the Internet. The family support worker obtains information from SENTASS, Contact a Family and educational psychologists.

The paediatric social workers say that information about welfare rights is important as it helps to fund parents to stay with their child in hospital and to support any other children at home. Information about health support services and educational special needs support is needed in preparation for the 'return home' phase of a child's care package. Information specifically about the names and roles of professionals who will work with the family at home is also seen as a part of service delivery.

Some of these workers raise issues about the role of information in the more general planning and delivery of services. Many workers from all professionals are keen to develop services that are 'evidenced-based' from research and best practice. To develop services in this manner brings to the fore the issue of the actual quality of information for the planning of services at various levels. As one social worker says, "information should inform strategic and operational planning; however the poor quality of the information we currently produce means that it only influences it".

Thus information does not only need to be accessible, clear and relevant, it also needs to be of good quality. A related issue to this is that there needs to be information that is 'authoritative' and 'official' so that both workers and parents (in their respective contexts) feel that they can trust it. This dimension raises the distinction between obtaining information through 'word of mouth' and from 'official' sources. Although parents and workers use word of mouth from their various peer support groups, they must have access to official information to be able to make informed decisions based on information that is authoritative.

Use of the guide

All these professionals have seen the guide. At the time of the guide's launch, copies had been sent to their respective departments and the Development Worker also distributed copies to workers.

The professionals promote the guide by giving out leaflets and by giving guides to parents and other professionals. They display posters, inform other members of staff and encourage them to attend 'guide training' sessions. The professionals are generally not aware if other professionals have copies of the guide. They do not know if it is easy for parents to obtain copies of the guide; however, they do tell parents about the guide. At present family support workers do not promote the guide because they do not currently have any children with disabilities attending their nursery.

The professionals, at present, do not use the guide with parents. Some use it to get telephone numbers to pass on to parents or just for themselves. Hospital based workers say it helps to raise parents' awareness of services before the child leaves hospital. They say that "although the guide is a useful tool, parents still want paid staff to guide them".

These workers think that the design of the guide is 'good', its layout is good and it is easy to use. The workers say that the sections are useful for finding out about health, education and so on. In particular the professionals think that the statutory or 'statutory led' services are outlined well. Workers make positive comments about the voluntary sector being listed alphabetically and they suggest that cross-referencing voluntary services with their own services might be a good idea for future editions. The rationale behind this is that this would help carers and workers to link the two to form a care package from community and social service provision.

Workers think that the guide is useful in raising awareness of the range of services and resources that are available for parents and children. However, these workers say parents need more than an information 'guide' to enable them to access services: parents also need personal support and advice. They do not know if parents find the guide useful as they have not worked with parents with the guide and they have not had any feedback about it. However, in general terms, they feel that the guide provides the kind of information that their service users need. It also provides information that the professionals did not know about. They think that the information is clear, concise and relevant. However, some of the information is deemed to be 'incorrect', which one professional says is to be expected in a first edition. Another professional states that the content is enough to help him/her contact services.

The workers feel that more information is needed on 'criteria for accessing services' and about what range of nursery provision is available. In relation to encouraging parents to use information and to contact services, one professional says that an 'advice line' contact is helpful. An advice line can bridge the gap between the written word and the spoken word in the 'stage of wondering', which involves a carer making the decision of whether or not to contact the service. This typically involves questions such as 'is this service for me?' or 'is this service for my child?'.

Information is seen as being powerful because it enables people to have fair access to services. Information for parents is seen as 'empowering' and is essential for workers. Professionals state that one of their main needs is to know where to find information, particularly when some information becomes out of date. These workers raise the issue of professionals all working in their own 'organisational boxes' with information maintained and contained in those boxes. They feel that it is important to open up access to information and they see the World Wide Web as one way to get out of 'organisational boxes'.

Health visitors

General roles and responsibilities, perceptions of information

The health visitors (who responded to the survey) work for Newcastle Primary Care NHS Trust. They work with other agencies in 'liaison' type relationships and the services they are in contact with include social services, education and voluntary agencies.

Their roles and responsibilities include:

- assessing health needs;
- planning and evaluating care and liaising with other agencies in the referral process;
- ensuring that families have up to date knowledge and information regarding health issues and what resources are available.

The health visitor's work with families includes conducting assessments, providing ongoing support and carrying out home visits. The nature of the work is characterised as being generalist and they continue to offer support to families after diagnosis and the introduction of appropriate services. They concentrate primarily on the child's needs. The frequency of contact with the child and family depends on the need and the nature of the problem. For example, parents of a new baby with disabilities can expect to have fortnightly visits.

The health visitors say they need information on what services are available, what services offer, information about benefits and information about particular conditions. They think that contact telephone numbers are important pieces of information. Their usual sources of information are paediatricians, social services and colleagues. They also use the Patient Information Centre, the Self-Help Directory and other local directories, the NHS Direct Health Information Line and directory enquiries. Other sources of information are members of the Children's Community Nursing Team and various support groups.

Health visitors think that information is an important part of their work because families look to professionals to provide up to date information. Giving information is seen as a large part of the health visitors' role. They feel that parents need information about their child's condition, about benefits and about other services, including support groups.

Use of the guide

All the health visitors have seen the guide and they obtain their copies through their professional networks, from the launch workshop and from the Patient Information Centre. They promote the guide by circulating leaflets, displaying posters, advising parents about it and generally by word of mouth.

One health visitor states that many parents have the guide, whereas other health visitors did not know if this was the case. The health visitors have mixed perceptions about how easy it is to obtain the guide, some think that it is 'easy to obtain' and others 'don't know'. They all, however, tell parents about the guide. One health visitor has had feedback about the guide from parents, which is very positive as parents say that the guide has an "easy format and they [parents] have been able to find information easily". Generally, health visitors find the guide useful and think it is easy to use and parent friendly.

Health visitors use the guide with parents as well as using it for themselves. They feel that it provides the information that is needed for their service users. It also provides the health visitors with information they did not know about. Examples of successful use include obtaining information about Disability North, welfare rights advice and information for a Disability Living Allowance application (that was successful). Further success includes using information in the guide to get in touch with the occupational therapy team at Shieldfield, which resulted in acquiring handrails for elderly clients. Health visitors say that it is still early days in the use of the guide but that they have used it approximately 20 times since its launch in February. They comment that up to date information is essential in service delivery.

Special Educational Needs Teaching and Support Service (SENTASS), Learning Support Manager, Careers Advisor

General roles and responsibilities, perceptions of information

All these professionals (who responded to the survey) work with other agencies in various ways. The SENTASS professionals are in contact with health colleagues such as paediatricians, health visitors, speech therapists, physiotherapists and the Community Team Learning Disability (CTLD). They are in contact with social workers and respite carers. They are also in touch with educational services, for example, Early Years, playgroups, nurseries, educational psychologists and primary schools, plus voluntary organisations.

The learning support managers are in contact with social services, the local education authorities and careers centres. They are also in contact with Rehab UK, Hunters Moore Rehabilitation Centre, Head Start, Northumberland Services for Head Injured People and Newcastle Society for the Blind.

The Careers Advisor works for the Tyneside Careers organisation. S/he makes referrals to youth training providers (work-based training for 16-19 year olds), to the Benefits Agency and to housing organisations.

The teachers working for SENTASS say that their roles and responsibilities are to:

- support the staff of the Young Children's Team;
- develop new ways of working and provide advice to the LEA;
- organise home teaching for pre-school children with Special Educational Needs (SEN);
- run groups for children and their families with a specific focus such as language, sensory and so on;
- provide support and advice to a range of 'early provision' services, for example, playgroups. SENTASS support the team of nursery nurses in the joint planning of programmes;
- contribute to the statutory assessment process leading to 'statements' of special needs;
- visit schools with parents to discuss support provision prior to a child's entry to reception school.

The roles and responsibilities of learning support managers include:

- assessing or arranging assessments of learning support needs for students who have learning difficulties and/or a disability;
- arranging support and coordinating any ensuing provision.

Careers advisors' roles and responsibilities include:

- working with 'statemented' pupils in mainstream schools;
- providing career guidance and supporting the transition from school to post-16 opportunities.

Teachers working with SENTASS explain the nature of their contact with families as conducting assessments, providing ongoing support, carrying out home visits, and some centre-based work. They see their role as one of being a specialist. They provide advice to the LEA about the needs of specific children and children in general. Their aim is to enable parents to become more effective teachers of their own children. The frequency of contact with families varies as 'every case is different' and the amount of intervention for each family varies depending on the needs of the child. However, a typical pattern of contact is an initial period of six-weekly home visits, followed by fortnightly visits augmented by attendance at groups.

Careers advisors' contact with children is often based at school, but they may have to be involved in visits to a child's home, with educational welfare officers, if the pupil is not attending school. They often work with school Special Educational Needs Co-ordinators (SENCOs) and participate in annual renewal statements with pupils in years 10 and 11 and the sixth form. They are mainly in contact with families at annual reviews, but parents are also invited into schools to attend careers interviews during year 10/11 or at the careers office at the 'post–16-years-old' stage. The learning support managers' contacts with families involve discussions with families of (usually) younger students to explore previous support and any support needs they might have at college. They also liaise with families, as needed, during the student's time at college.

Teachers state that they need personal information about a child, including date of birth, address and diagnosis (if known), and which professionals are involved in the care of the child. They need information about the home situation, which they usually get through their contact with the families. They need access to professional knowledge of the child, with reference to development and conditions. They need information about the facilities available and ways to access them, and information about statutory regulations. They want general information about benefits, about specific conditions/disabilities and information about other services with contact names and numbers.

Their usual sources of information are EYDCP (Early Years Development and Childcare Partnership) and the Children's Information Service, paediatricians, physiotherapists and speech therapists. Other sources include Contact a Family, Disability North, and the Children with Disability Service. Further sources are the educational department, educational psychologists, SENTASS colleagues, schools and voluntary organisations, such as the National Autistic Society, Down's Syndrome Association and Scope.

Learning support managers require information in 'as much detail as possible' and 'as early as possible' to plan appropriate support in terms of staffing and equipment. Their sources of information are personal networks, conferences, books and magazines, the Internet and material updates from organisations and suppliers. Careers advisors say that they need accurate up to date information on career progression and opportunities from

five

organisations that help disabled young people. In this context they think the guide is very useful. Their other sources of information are publicised careers information, books and the Internet.

These professionals, as a group, think that parents need information relating to every aspect of a child's disability. This includes how the disability may develop and how it may affect the life of the child and the family. Parents need to know what services are available and where to go for urgent help. They should also be aware of parent support groups and any other relevant voluntary organisations. Families need to know how they can best support their children, which also includes knowing about benefits, aids and adaptations. Parents also need to understand any legal aspects of care such as 'statementing' in education. However, the professionals state that information should be given in an appropriate manner and a source person or agency should always be known to be available.

These professionals agree with the professionals in previous sections – information is seen as central to their role.

Use of the guide

This group of professionals say exactly the same things about the guide as the professionals cited in the previous categories. However, they do raise some additional points. One professional suggests that 'loose leaf' might be a better design option for the guide because it would be cheaper and easier to keep up to date (as separate pages could be printed off when required rather than a whole book). One source of access that has not been mentioned by the workers in the previous categories is that the guide was available to users and workers in what they termed their 'group room'.

In relation to feedback from parents, these professionals say that parents find the guide useful. They sometimes find that parents forget about the guide until a professional brings it out; this indicates that parents in their search for information do not, as yet, automatically use the guide.

One professional is concerned that sometimes professionals may only paint half the picture, which means that some workers may be selective about what information parents are given. Although s/he notes that it would be inappropriate to bombard parents with too much information, checks should be in place to ensure parents get the 'whole picture'. The same professional states that "access to information is one of the most difficult issues to deal with". S/he welcomes the post-launch research and hopes that the guide is distributed to those without normal access to services, such as parents who may have a disability and not know of the guide's existence.

Paediatricians

General roles and responsibilities, perceptions of information

The two paediatricians (who responded to the survey) work for Newcastle Hospitals NHS Trust. In general, one paediatrician is involved with other services outside of hospitals, whereas the other is not. The paediatrician who is involved with other services works with social services. Their roles and responsibilities include:

- detection of actual or potential disability in children;
- medical care and assessment of children;
- providing care in the areas of specialist neonatal, general paediatrics and disability.

The nature of their contact with families involves conducting assessments, providing support and making initial diagnoses and statements. Where multiple specialities are involved, they coordinate health involvement. One of the consultants says s/he is happy to do care planning in the client's homes or other venues. One of them oversees children with Down's Syndrome and provides Down's Syndrome guidelines. The timing of contact with families varies from monthly to annually, and they try to make contact as regularly as possible.

The paediatricians state that they need information about the other agencies that are involved with a specific child, including the names of the professionals involved. Their usual sources of information are parents, letters (including copies from other professionals) and the guide. Further sources include Contact a Family, the Internet, textbooks and colleagues.

Paediatricians say that parents need information about diagnosis (if any) and its meaning and likely outcome(s), or at least prospects for the near future. Parents also need information about 'who can help', such as agencies and groups that offer support outside medical services, health services and social services.

The paediatricians think that information is "pretty crucial" in the provision of services, but it is difficult to be very specific about it. Networking with the care team is thought to be vital. Ensuring that parents have access to information is thought to be very important. Paediatricians say that helping parents to interpret the information is one of their major roles.

Use of the guide

The paediatricians have seen the guide and they found out about it through professional networks. They obtained their copies through a professional network and from the Development Worker. They promote it by circulating leaflets, posters, by word of mouth recommendation, and by putting a "stack of copies into the Child Development Centre".

five

Generally, they do not know how many parents and professionals have the guide. They think that professionals have easy access to the guide. One tells parents about the guide, but the other does not. They have not had any feedback from parents about the guide.

One paediatrician thinks the guide is an "important part of a big enterprise in helping parents access information"; the other paediatrician thinks it is "probably useful". They think that the design of the guide is "very sound". They both think that the guide provides the sort of information that parents need. One paediatrician says the guide provides him/her with information that s/he had not known about, whereas the other paediatrician did not find any new information.

They feel that the guide has been well prepared, but they cannot comment on the accuracy of the information; however, quality and format is fine. One of the paediatrician's thinks that the Internet could form a good parallel to the guide and other information sources by providing real-time updates.

Ethnic minority voluntary sector worker

In order to gain some understanding of the role of information and the use of the guide for Asian families with children with disabilities, a worker in the voluntary sector who works with Asian carers, and who is Asian, was interviewed.

The worker explained that research carried out by social workers nine years ago highlights the importance of having an Asian Carers Project. The research shows that many Asian families live in the most deprived areas of the community and that they generally do not have enough access to information. Thus, when Asian carers live in deprived areas, have difficulties with the English language, and cope with depression and anxiety (often associated with having a disabled child), it makes it four times more difficult for them to go out and get information than it is for their white counterparts.

The worker says that s/he took up the post nine years ago and developed networks and information resources. S/he explains that it is a two-way process, in that other professionals and workers publicise the voluntary sector service and refer families to the service and s/he puts families in contact with the other services. S/he says that "at the beginning of the Asian Carers Project the professionals benefited from our service because before they were not sure if the families were getting what they needed, maybe because of language barriers and so on".

General roles and responsibilities, perceptions of information

The main part of the worker's job is to link families with other services, support families through formal counselling and provide a listening service. The worker says that many families are now fairly independent in gaining information and that they are becoming quite empowered in seeking services. However, carers are still getting what s/he calls "very broken services". S/he helps them to coordinate their care and tries to make sure that families are getting everything they need, including helping them to use information to improve their quality of life. The Asian Carers Project worker's responsibilities are not as well defined as those of workers in the more mainstream professions such as nurses, for example. The worker's more broadly defined responsibility facilitates a more holistic, general and flexible service that is tailored to the specific circumstances of the child, family and carers living in Asian communities.

Use of the guide

The worker says that s/he found out about the guide at the launch and training day. In general, s/he thinks the guide is "quite a good thing but parents are not going to use it". S/he says that the project workers have developed their own networks and it is these networks that are the most valuable for parents. S/he comments that "we use this guide very little at the moment", although they sometimes get phone calls from people who have seen things in the guide. The worker sees the project's networks and meeting place as very important in providing information

by the 'drop-ins' and advice sessions. S/he comments, "I am not saying that we don't need any information but we need more staff and things like that. Sometimes you collect information, but don't use that information". The worker and staff get information via their networks, from leaflets, social services, charities and other professionals who send information to them. They do not use the Internet or computers to get information.

The worker comments on the importance of communication with families and other professionals. S/he says that communication directly with families, in relation to information, support and advice is much more important than using the Internet or listening to recorded messages on health information lines. In some cases s/he thinks the telephone is very useful; s/he prefers to communicate with families by talking to them face to face (at the centre or in a family home) or by telephone. S/he feels that individual needs are very important, especially with relation to disability, because each disability is different for each child and all children have different needs. Even if children with disabilities have a similar background, their needs can be totally different. The worker thinks 'trust' is important in relation to information and support and says of the service that "families know that what they are saying is confidential. It is not going to go out of these four walls and they can talk about anything. If there is action to be taken then the workers take it, and as project workers they try to help in any way".

five

S/he cites Contact a Family as "a very good organisation". S/he says, "although Contact a Family is dealing mainly with English mothers, they have a lot of similar concerns to our mothers". The worker comments that it is more difficult for Asian mothers and s/he tells the following story to highlight cultural differences that compound the difficulties experienced through disability.

"There was a time when someone wanted to take a child away for a week's holiday. The person speaking to me was a white man. So before trying to persuade the mother to let her disabled daughter go on this holiday break I want to make sure that a female will be going. The mother trusts me so much. She says if you think that is OK then I will let my daughter go. So I mentioned this to her teacher as well. I said I would appreciate it if a female were involved as well. When the mother is putting so much trust in me it makes me feel a little uncomfortable, especially when he keeps contacting me to persuade mum to make her decision. It is a very good opportunity for this girl to go. When I speak to some of the white mothers they say it will be the same for us, we have the same concerns about our learning disabled daughters. We think they should be in the company of a female teacher. So there are some similarities but I think the white mothers will go to school and find out more. So this is putting me in a very difficult position. I can't really make these journeys to school all the time, although I do it sometimes. But I think the school should do something to alleviate the worries of the families. They should visit the families with me to build confidence and trust."

The worker says that s/he had told other agencies:

"If you really want to include the Asian community, then employ a social worker that is Asian. So if they have to travel somewhere with them in a taxi, they are with someone who knows their language, someone who has familiarity with their own food or something like that. They are worried that no one from the Asian community is using this service and employing an Asian worker would help this. It is like a 4- or 5-year-old child starting school. They feel like a total stranger amongst all these new people. It is the same for an Asian who is 25 going to a group of strangers not knowing their language and not understanding their culture. It can be very intimidating."

In many ways the situation of Asian children with disabilities is one of being 'doubly excluded', first because of the difference between Asian culture and mainstream English culture and second because of their disability. From this perspective, although the guide is welcomed, the emphasis on the provision of information is based on communicative networks via face-to-face meetings, telephone calls, home visits and drop-in sessions. Trust is important, as is an understanding of, and respect, for Asian cultures as they all interact with the meanings of disability. Information is important to the families, but it needs to be delivered in ways that are appropriate given the situations of some of these families. However, in the nine years of the project, experience also shows that some families are now managing their own information searches.

Some responses about the guide from feedback forms

The responses from workers who completed a form in the guide reinforce the general response from the survey. The comments on the forms say that there is the right amount of information in the guide, and that it is "excellent", "concise" and "easy to read".

However, the respondents have some concerns. One issue is that information about housing needs to be improved. Another point is that information about equipment might be useful in future editions. A suggestion by one person is that private sector providers need to be included so those parents who receive direct payments have the information to make choices about which services to buy. In relation to the professionals, one person asks why GPs are not in the directory. These points are all open to debate. As **Chapter three** of this report shows, decisions have to be made about the format of any guide, which involves making some compromises in relation to its intended function.

Nonetheless, comments by various workers in information services suggest that there is an appropriate balance of information in the design of the guide. One manager of an information service says "I think the guide's great – not too bulky, a good layout, easy to read etc". Comments by managers from some of the major service providers are also positive. The comments support the general tone of the research about the early use of the guide, which is that the guide is a tool that is really needed in the general provision of services for parents with disabled children. Furthermore, the guide is a useful tool for workers and professionals in the field of services for parents with disabled children.

Summary and analysis of research with professionals

The number of professionals and workers who are involved with the care of disabled children is an indication of the complexity of the needs of disabled children. The professionals all bring a different perspective to the issue of information in the provision of services; nonetheless, they all see information as important to their work. In general terms, the workers think that the guide is well designed, easy to use and a useful tool for parents of disabled children. Broadly speaking, workers say that parents need information about what services are available and what they do, how to access services, benefit entitlements, and what workers' roles and responsibilities are. They say that parents need information about community and peer support groups, about transition times in a child's life, where to go in a crisis, and information about diagnosis.

five

Use of information

Although the workers all agree that the provision of information is important in their practice, the way workers use information is complex. Each worker uses information in a slightly different way in relation to their respective roles and responsibilities, and they need different information in view of these roles. A further complexity to this is the development of a multi-agency service that is tending to work more with a social definition of disability to address the holistic needs of a disabled child. There is, therefore, both a need for specialist professional information and for more general community-based information. Linked to this is the issue that all professionals give information to parents in slightly different ways given the context of their professional practice. These points have implications for: 1) designing information; and 2) judging the appropriateness of the information at the different stages of a child's condition, in the different aspects of a child's condition, and in different contexts. One of the consequences of this is that we need to understand the comments of the professionals in this report in relation to their respective perspectives.

There are, however, several overarching themes:

1)   Information is an important aspect of service delivery. Information has several roles: it helps workers and professionals to do their work; it is needed for operational and strategic planning of services; and information can empower parents to seek the best possible service for their children.

2)   All workers develop their own ways of obtaining information, which comprises their own networks and other official sources such as libraries, the Internet, professional courses, and so on.

3)   Workers want the best for service users and want their service (in some form) to be 'user centred'.

4)   All workers give information to parents from their perspective in relation to their role in the child's care. Workers have, however, an understanding that parents need a broad range of information to help them with all aspects of a child's disability.

5)   Many workers recognise that for a lot of parents, access to appropriate information is not easy or even possible. Workers are therefore, to one degree or another, aware that the information needs of parents are not being met, and they offer insights into what is important about information from their own point of view.

Providing information to parents/ carers

The ethnic voluntary worker stresses the issue of trust and good communication skills in the giving of information to parents. S/he also raises the issue that information needs to be available in different languages and that face-to-face meetings are important in helping parents and carers to understand information. One danger of this approach is that parents may rely on one source of information; however, this does not seem to be the case as many Asian carers are now independent in accessing information and services. The worker also acts as a link person between agencies, an example of some sort of informal key working activity.

Paediatricians raise the issue of information about diagnosis, its meaning and any likely outcomes. They feel that it is important to ensure parents have access to any relevant information, and they see one of their major roles as helping parents to interpret the information. As the guide is designed to act as a signpost for information about services, it does not directly address the information needs of parents about diagnosis: the guide therefore highlights an unmet need of information about diagnosis. This relates to the point that context is important; for example, paediatric social workers say that parents need information about hospital accommodation so parents can stay with their children while the child is in hospital.

Another important context and stage for carers and children is the move from hospital to home, and paediatric social workers and health visitors stress the need for information to support this transition.

These examples show that information and the giving of information needs to be sensitive to the context and specific needs of carers.

In the more community-based services such as the Children's Community Nurses, social workers and specialist health nurses, family support workers and so on, the emphasis is on information helping carers to facilitate and improve the quality of life of their children. These workers think that information is important in two ways,

apart from their actual practice-based information needs. First, they need information about other services in the community as well as in their own immediate professional networks so that they can help carers to access all the services that carers need. Although, to a degree, they have a specific role as, for example nurses, as *community* nurses they also have to be able to give information about other services (schools, housing, self-help groups and so on). Second, they need information so that they can develop 'evidenced-based' services, especially as many of the community workers are developing a multi-agency service. The workers in the community say that the guide is a good first step and is useful to them as they work in the community; it forms a link for them with other services as well as helping carers to construct a care package for their children.

However, some professionals (see in particular the **SENTASS** section on pages 54-56) recognise access to information is one of the most difficult issues in service provision. Some workers are concerned that parents do not get all the information they need and that sometimes professionals may be selective about what information they give to parents, thus depriving carers of a more comprehensive picture. Although workers say that care has to be taken to ensure that carers are not overloaded with information, nonetheless, checks need to be put in place to make sure that carers have all the information they need. Workers in the field of information services support this point and broaden it by saying that parents/carers have wide and varying information needs. This report shows that it is not only what

five

information carers get, when and why, that is important, but also how they get it. Information workers argue that parents want a single human contact for their information needs with flexible access to electronic and hard copy information sources. This piece of research shows how complex the service environment is and how complex the needs of disabled children are. This seems to support one information worker's view that it is important to offer a single-entry access point to parents, such as the guide.

Use of the guide

To help meet the information needs of parents, most of the workers promote and distribute the guide. Although the guide is still in early use, many workers are beginning to use it. Many professionals are in some sense 'experimenting' with the guide to see how they can use it within their current practice, as well as seeing how it might improve their practise. They are also in the process of finding out about the best ways to use the guide with parents and so are being sensitive to issues such as developing trust, helping parents to interpret information and supporting parents in doing their own information seeking. Most workers are doing this from their own perspectives, so there is an unevenness of development of use of the guide. For example, the Asian voluntary sector worker is not making much use of the guide because s/he values face-to-face meetings or talking on the telephone. On the other hand, the community nurses are using the guide more often, as they are finding that it is helping them to supply community-type information to the carers they work with.

There is, therefore, a balance to be struck between enabling carers to find information, which has the potential to empower them and the more direct role of supporting carers in understanding the information, without depriving carers of their ability to make their own decisions. Early use of the guide suggests that it is a tool for workers to help coordinate services, albeit, as yet, in a very basic way by helping to link services and build rapport between workers, carers and other agencies in the construction of care networks. Yet, the guide also gives parents an independent source of information to help them check that they are getting access to services and other sources of support. The guide can therefore act as a check in making sure that parents are getting all the information they need, rather than relying on information selected by a worker.

However, most workers welcome the guide. They see it as a well designed information tool for carers and for themselves. Many professionals are, however, in the process of finding out how best to use it in their everyday practice.

Conclusions

The research into the development and early use of the guide identifies five key themes in relation to the guide, information and the joining up of services.

These are:

- a general evaluation of the guide;
- understanding information in a broad sense;
- understanding the contexts of the use of information;
- designing information;
- the life of the guide.

The conclusion discusses each of these themes and finishes with a summary.

General evaluation of the guide: did the guide achieve what it set out to do?

The research indicates that the guide has fulfilled what the developers of the guide wanted to achieve. As **Chapter three** of the report shows, the 'developers' identified that parents need to know what services exist and how to access them. Furthermore, there was not one easily accessible source of information for parents of disabled children about local services. They therefore decided to produce a guide that would provide basic information about local community services and would act as a signpost to other sources of more detailed information. The guide was not intended to meet all the information needs of parents and neither would it be the only way for parents to access information: it was simply to be **one source of information** that would work with other sources of information. A further objective of producing the guide was to help 'kick-start' a more planned and systematic approach to the provision of information. It was also hoped that this process would help to identify areas of unmet need. In relation to the design, the first edition of the guide aimed to be 'easy to use' and 'fit for purpose'. The use of the guide has brought to the fore many other issues about providing information.

In general terms, parents welcome the guide and think that the design of it makes it easy to use. Parents see the guide as an excellent tool to help them become *aware* of local services and thus, with the practical information in the guide, help them to *access* local services. They are pleased to have information about local services in one guide. The use of the guide by parents has identified some unmet needs. One is that parents need information at the 'pre-diagnosis' stage of beginning to recognise that a child might have some impairment. Parents say that it is often difficult to get a child's condition recognised and without a condition being recognised they cannot access many of the support services.

Professionals also welcome the guide as a useful tool for carers and for themselves. They think that is it **a well designed, easy to use source of information to find out about community services**. In general terms they think that the guide provides the type of information that parents need. Some of the workers who operate in the community find it useful: it gives them information about other services in the community with which to inform carers and to help with any emerging multi-agency service. They suggest some minor amendments that they think might improve the guide, such as more information about 'very local services', more cross-referencing of information, and that SSHNs should be mentioned in the introductions to both the health *and* education sections. These comments are useful but they need to be considered in the full design process. An unmet information need identified by professionals is that **parents need appropriate information about all aspects of diagnosis**.

The guide has achieved its objective; it provides one good quality source of 'signposting' information about local services that is easy to use. Some suggestions by parents and workers will inform the design of future editions. In the design and early use of the guide, research identifies some unmet needs, which form subjects for future research. The research about the design and the use of the guide also raises many wider issues about information. The authors' concluding point is that although the guide is good it must be understood as a tool in a broader information environment. To maximise the potential of the guide both for carers as they seek information and for service providers in the drive for quality and efficient services, **the guide needs to be situated in the broader dynamics of services and the various situations of carers**.

Understanding information in a broad sense

Through the process of developing an information guide and the post-launch research, several key issues emerge. Broadly speaking, the developers of the guide have been successful in responding to what parents said they wanted, in identifying areas of unmet information need and areas for further research. However, through the development and post-launch research, clarity of some of the most significant issues for parents emerged. This is important in understanding information within the dynamics of service provision and family care.

Although parents are pleased to have a new source of information, they are nonetheless concerned about the adequacy of current service provision. A major concern among parents is that **many services do not have sufficient resources to meet demand**, which often results in long waiting lists. Furthermore, the lack of resources impacts on the quality of the service, which is reflected not only in the level of care but also in the quality of information that professionals give to carers.

Parents are also concerned about the lack of multi-agency services and the lack of 'joined up' working by professionals. They indicate that they are pleased to get information, but because the needs of disabled children are so complex and involve so many agencies, they would welcome some support in coordinating a child's care package. The nature of that support is open to debate. Nonetheless, there seems to be a need for some form of key working or care coordination to enable parents to make choices about a myriad of services, and for services to be able to respond to that choice in a coordinated manner. Furthermore, many parents do not mind professionals sharing information about their child if it means that children get the care they need. Many parents feel that the major service providers should have a 'process' for the exchange of information; for example, 'fieldworkers' to channel information from the hospital to the school. Parents raise a related aspect in that they feel that services either do not or cannot respond to their needs, so parents often feel that they have to 'fight' to get through 'barriers' to get the appropriate care for their child.

A second dimension to the broader aspects of information in service environments is concerned with the dynamics of inclusion and exclusion. This relates to the issue of getting a child's condition formally recognised so that s/he can access services. Although the practice of having criteria of access to service acts to help allocate services to those in need, often the fact that children have to meet certain 'criteria' for getting access to services can contribute to producing exclusion. In some cases a child's needs might not be understood and parents have to 'fight' to get their child's condition recognised so that they can access services. In other cases, having a child's condition 'statemented' can be stigmatising. These raise issues in the development of multi-agency service, which aims to meet the holistic needs of a disabled child in a social model of disability. Thus, there needs to be a way to provide specialist care and added support so that children with impairments can participate fully in everyday life in ways that are not stigmatising. In this context both workers and carers need relevant information to coordinate and support this aspiration. This point raises questions about the role of information, and suggests that **forms of information interact with issues of access and eligibility in rather complex ways that, as yet, we do not understand**.

These broader issues highlight the complexity of developing information and services in ways that are inclusive and enabling for all children in our society. A conclusion from this argument is that information requires to be understood in relation to service provision and user need, and be designed to be useful within these dynamics. Thus, although information is seen as important to carers so that they can exercise choice, the actual practice of exercising choice is not straightforward in the current organisation of welfare. This, in turn, suggests the need to unpack what information means, and as a first step to understand how information is being used.

six

Understanding the contexts of the use of information

One of the overriding themes to emerge from the research is the complexity of the needs of disabled children and the coterminous complex service environment. This complex environment is experienced by many parents as 'disjointed' or 'fragmented', at levels of finding out about services, other general informational needs, and the actual coordination of care packages. Professionals also find the environment complex: they are aware of the holistic needs of a disabled child, which is now also being reflected in emerging multi-agency service provision. The section about professionals shows, however, that the diverse range of roles and responsibilities of workers involved with disabled children makes coordination of services difficult.

The research confirms the difficulties that parents have in accessing the information they need. As **Chapter three** shows, many parents are aware of what they want information about and can make suggestions about the form of that information. They are, however, unclear about how to access and use information. For example, they welcome the guide as a tool (clear and easy to use), but are as yet uncertain about how it will help them: the guide is not yet established in the ways they usually seek information. At present many parents find out about services and benefits in an *ad hoc* fashion. Parents develop 'information seeking' skills through experience, with many however, not getting the services and support they need while they 'are learning'. Carers sometimes feel that professionals do not give them all the information they need, therefore trust needs to be established between carers and professionals. Both formal and informal social networks are important sources through which carers find information and learn to use information.

If information is to empower carers then there must be a more systematic provision of information with overarching training about information seeking. Furthermore, parents need to find out about information in ways that are sensitive to their situation. Thus, for example, an Asian carer without English as a first language may want the services of an Asian carer centre with face-to-face support. Parents whose child has just been diagnosed may require the paediatrician to explain what the diagnosis means, and a carer wanting to find out about community services may want the guide. It is important that parents feel empowered to care for their child by the way information is exchanged. Workers, therefore, need to be open about the information they give, saying if they are being selective, answering questions and expanding on any information, and pointing parents to other sources of information.

These points raise the issue of the role of professionals and agencies involved in the care of disabled children and how they perceive and use information. The authors found that workers tended to use information in slightly different ways given their specific role and responsibilities. Also, given emerging multi-agency service provision, there is a need for specialist professional information and boarder community-based information. However, the authors found that many workers are learning to use the guide in their everyday practice, and that many workers are aware that information is an important part of service provision, albeit a 'very difficult' part of it. Generally workers meet their information needs from a variety of sources; however, further work needs to be done to see if a more coherent information source for workers can be constructed, particularly for emerging multi-agency service.

The context in which information is used is one of changing environments. From a policy perspective, service users such as carers should be able to exercise choice for which they need information. This, however, is a cultural change from the more traditional relationship users had with welfare services, which was generally more paternalistic. However, the emerging carer-as-consumer and the new orientation of exercising choice in negotiating welfare, require training. Furthermore, not all users are equally empowered to seek information; often the multidimensionality of caring for a disabled child puts constraints on carers' information seeking activities. Workers are also experiencing change, with many of them developing and working in multi-agency service environments. This, along with the drive to develop 'user-centred' service, is raising various issues around the nature and provision of information in everyday professional practice.

At present there is some evidence of a lack of clarity about how to use information and what information is needed to address the needs of disabled children in the social model. Many workers are thinking through issues surrounding information and are combining old ways of using information with new ways to meet emerging demands. The multidisciplinary workshops organised by the NSNN Development Worker are one example of improving the use of information by workers. However, further training for workers may help them to develop new information skills in their everyday practice of caring for disabled children.

This discussion highlights that there are complex cultural changes occurring around the needs of disabled children, and that the ways in which information is understood, used and developed is undergoing change, both by parents and professionals. There are therefore **issues of strategic planning and change management** to ensure that this cultural change is supported by organisational and informational change. The development of information needs to be supported by training for parents and workers about using information. Additionally any development should be informed by research to make sure that information is shaped to meet the needs of parents and workers, as services undergo change.

six

Designing information

The design of information is complex, and one of the key themes to emerge out of this work is that design is a 'process'. The process has several dimensions: research, the design of a product such as a guide, the development of social networks, and the involvement of key groups.

The role of interagency development workers is important in the design of information; they have the ability to conduct research to discover other approaches to design and to develop networks to facilitate design at a local, regional and national level. Furthermore, they can plan and manage the whole process of designing information – from proof of concept to publicity and distribution of the final product. As stated in **Chapter three**, this is a complex process where a balance between an information source being well researched and yet still remaining up to date has to be achieved.

In designing an actual product there are aspects of design such as 'good practice' guidelines that are already available and proven, and these are useful to draw on. However, part of the design process involves considering what the specific function of information is; for example, in this case a signposting guide, who the target audience is, what type of information, and so on. This involves bringing together a steering group (design team) so that these design decisions can be discussed.

A key conclusion from the authors' work in Newcastle upon Tyne is that **good design needs to be based on 'partnership working', involving various professionals and carers**. The Development Worker is key in this process, and **Chapter three** gives examples of professionals working together at different stages in the design and production process. This chapter shows that the process involves workers with a variety of skills coming together at the appropriate stage to take parts of the work forward, for example, the PR's forum and the work on publicity. The work of designing and producing the guide involved approximately 90 people. **A main conclusion is that the design, production and distribution of the guide could not have succeeded, especially within the available timescale, had good working relationships and clarity of tasks not been established**.

The steering group made every effort to include carers in the design process, and the group feels that they managed to include views of carers. However, from their experience members of the steering group say that it is not easy to include carers in design processes because many carers face constraints to participation. There is a lack of understanding of how to incorporate carers' views into design. Therefore, despite the best efforts to involve parents, the lesson members of the steering group have learned is that, as yet, they do not fully understand how to do this.

An overriding consideration of what this means for designing information is that **design is a continual learning process**. There are certain proven tools and guidelines available, which can be used in the design process. These, however, have to be adapted to suit the specific information source that is being produced. This point leads to the critical factor in producing information 'fit for purpose', which is **the development of social networks** that are relevant to the information product being produced. The respective members of these networks need to have the appropriate knowledge and skills to inform aspects of the design process. This, however, is not a straightforward process. Nonetheless, if information is to be useful, in some sense 'timely and appropriate' for specific and/or general purpose, then the meaning of the information for those using it must constantly be addressed. To achieve this purpose, to any degree, requires the **development of partnerships to inform the process of design**.

The life of the guide

The overarching conclusion is that the guide is an **excellent first step in the development of information for carers of disabled children**. However, there are many issues to address in any further development of information.

At the moment, the guide is not an automatic part of the ways in which carers find out about information and services. The guide is at a stage of early use, and it needs time to become embedded in any information seeking activity. However,

early use indicates that it has had a positive response by carers and workers and is meeting a demand. Further editions would help establish the value of this form of information for carers and services. The guide needs time to become incorporated into the usual ways parents and workers seek information. One worker, for example, says that at the moment often "parents forget they have the guide". There needs to be **ongoing evaluation** of the guide to assess its value to carers and service providers as the guide becomes more established, as well as to evaluate any changes made to its design.

Any further development of the guide involves considering two issues: 1) the specific details of producing a second edition; and 2) the wider multi-agency agenda.

There are several points about the production of this first edition of the guide that relate to the specific details of producing a second edition. The first edition was developed out of the recognition of the need for the post of Development Worker to facilitate multi-agency service planning and provision for disabled children. The post was a joint-funded inter-agency post (health and social services) and was part of the 'joined up working' agenda. The post, however, ceased to exist at the end of October 2001. The characteristics of the guide reflect the multi-agency nature of the Development Worker post; the guide gives information about many services and cuts across many agencies in the statutory and voluntary sector. This multi-agency work has produced a multi-agency product – a signposting guide to local services.

six

71

Therefore, if another edition is to be produced it will have to be situated in multi-agency service development; it cannot sit in any one agency. A multi-agency team (steering group) must inform the development of the design process. Furthermore, our experience shows that the **production of a guide is best achieved through commissioning a specialist organisation**.

The second consideration is the relationship between the development of a multi-agency strategy and providing information for carers of disabled children. This involves gaining a greater clarity about the ways in which agencies can work together, which includes debates about issues such a key working and the nature of key working. Any multi-agency strategy needs to consider what the information needs of workers and carers might be as multi-agency service evolves. It also needs to ask how workers use information and how that impacts on carers in various ways. Another aspect of joining up that relates to information is the issue of carers having a single point of access to information. Further work is needed here to assess the advantages of such a facility, and what developments would need to occur to build such a facility. Related work is also needed about other sources of generic and specific information sources in the city to ascertain what a coherent information strategy might look like to support multi-agency service provision. **This may well involve unpacking issues about one-stop shops**.

Summary

The first edition of the guide has identified many aspects of what a guide that supplies information about local community services and is a signpost to other information should 'look like'. The production of the guide provided many valuable insights into the processes of producing information. The development of a guide and the evaluation of its early use have enabled researchers to explore the broader dynamics of providing quality information in changing service environments. These areas are important as they can inform future developments of information and service provision to meet the needs of service users and service providers. At the applied level the needs of carers are particularly complex and the guide has gone some way to meeting their information needs. **In general terms the guide is an excellent first step in developing a more coherent and accessible information service to meet the needs of carers and workers in the still evolving multi-agency environment of welfare provision**.

Lessons for groups wanting to create an information guide of local services

Involving user groups and professionals

- A steering group is important, with approximately five participants. The group should consist of parents and workers from voluntary and statutory agencies. It should be facilitated by a development worker, and members need experience of information provision and direct work with families of disabled children.

- The guide should provide information that will 'signpost' parents and professionals to relevant services to meet need. The information should be provided in a user-friendly and concise way.

- Feedback at the draft stage is essential. The feedback required is on accuracy of details and to identify any omissions, and agreement on the contents list and order of sections, as well as general comments about the 'feel' of the guide and ease of reading.

Managing the process

- Because the information for the guide comes from many local and national sources it is important to have a link person such as an interagency development worker.

Researching similar publications

- Lessons learnt in this project included a requirement to understand local needs, that there needs to be absolute clarity about the aim of the information, and that is it impossible to include all services in one guide. A guide must therefore be a 'starting point' for parents to search for more detailed information.

Production

- The steering group advised the use of an experienced service provider in the production of a guide. Such a provider may add value, in this case through their expertise in researching and producing health and social care directories.

- A task checklist is vital to monitor process and coordinate activity (see the example on page 21).

Design

- Main points in regard to accessibility are that the guide should be easy to read and use, jargon free, clear and concise, and contain sufficient information in each of the entries to trigger a response by the user.

- To ensure good specification (see the example on pages 20-21) there should be a steering group that involves parents and professionals. It is also important to identify common themes and to make use of some specialist service provider expertise.

- There may be budgetary constraints that require decisions to be made about resources. Ensuring a good specification, as noted in the above point, makes efficient use of resources.

six

Promoting the guide

- A strategy involving various media is recommended. A local service PR group is useful and can access local and regional newspapers.
- Leaflets, posters, informal promotion and articles are all important in raising awareness of the guide.
- Practitioner workshops are an excellent forum in which to launch and promote a guide and to further educate workers in the provision of information.

Use of the guide

- The information team at PIC identified a number of themes in relation to the guide. Many callers appeared to think that they needed 'permission' from a professional before asking for a copy of guide and some parents were not sure what they were asking for. Members of the information team should find a way to reassure parents that the guide is free.
- *Users responses:* Users saw the guide of this project as a good 'first step' in the development of information of local services. They recognised that the function of the guide is one of 'signposting', which enables users to find out what services are available and how to access them. Users found the guide easy to use – the size of the guide makes it easy to handle, the print is clear and the topic sections are helpful.
- *Professionals' responses:* Professionals all bring a different perspective to the issue of information in the provision of services; nonetheless, this report has shown that they all view information and the provision of information as important in their work. In this project, the professionals thought that the guide was well designed, easy to use and a useful tool for parents of disabled children. The various professionals use information in different ways, however, the development of multi-agency work has led to professional demand for both specialised information and general community-based information.

This project indicates that to produce an effective guide to services a good steering group and social network are essential. Producing the specifications and the guide is a process that needs to be managed by a link person. The guide also needs to be well publicised to raise awareness of it in parent and service provider communities.

seven

Recommendations for further research and for policy

Understanding the use of information by parents and professionals

1) What is available for families and where from? How do they know what is available including the availability and accessibility of information for parents whose first language is not English?

2) We know more about the role of workers, but are they empowering, enabling, or producing barriers to information?

3) More research is needed to get a clearer picture about parents' wishes to manage (control) their own information gathering (with appropriate tools):
   - Should or could a worker do this?
   - Should it be all workers or a 'key worker'?

   and/or
   - Should there be a robust/accessible information system for all parents (not solely those of disabled children) to support a more inclusive approach?

4) The guide *does not* set out to tell parents:
   - what they are entitled to;
   - give detailed information about benefits;
   - give information about disability or diagnosis.

However, the research highlights that these are areas of unmet information need. Further research is needed to explore these areas and identify appropriate ways of informing carers about these aspects of disability.

5) More specifically if parents need advice at the 'wondering stage' then:
   - Whose role is it to give this advice?
   - Would another 'advice line' be the answer?

Joining up – how to do it

- We know more about the information needs of workers and how they meet them, and that there are gaps and the guide filled one of these gaps. But what are their evolving information needs?
- Are agencies working together? Who should work together? How should they work together?
- Are there generic or specific information points in the city and where are these? For example, the Customer Service Centre (Civic Centre), Patient Information Centre, NHS Direct, Carers Information Point. Do any or all of these see themselves as one-stop shops? Who do they 'serve'? What are their plans for development? How may they fit into multi-agency developments?
- There is a need to clarify and map 'who' is currently involved in collating/ providing/distributing information (and of what type and format) and the relationships that exist between these providers.
- Who are the target audiences for information? Are the different audiences comprised of parents/carers, workers, planners, and/or children? If so, what are their respective needs?
- It is likely that a separate piece of work will need to be undertaken to ensure we understand the issues concerning information needs/provision for the children themselves.

Further work is needed to understand the possible characteristics of key working and one-stop shops in relation to multi-agency service and the provision of information.

Policy recommendations

1) To overcome the various impacts of cultural change in service delivery it is recommended that information training for carers and workers is developed and provided.

2) It is important to understand the context of information use so that information can be designed to meet these specific contexts.

3) It is important to have a design strategy for information so that information needs are identified across agencies to meet holistic need. The strategy also needs to ensure that information is part of the development of services and is part of carers' coping strategies.

4) It is recommended that all information tools are assessed within the broad information strategy to identify gaps, to maximise coordination of information and to help identify training needs.

5) The needs of disabled children and their carers are multidimensional, requiring forms of multi-agency service, so information must reflect this and cater for these needs.

6) Agencies and organisations need to see information as an asset and thus integral in planning processes. It is recommended that interagency development posts be continued.

7) Social networks are central in the design processes of a guide and in publicising and training activities.

8) There is a need to design an underpinning infrastructure for information to meet the needs of holistic care and multi-agency service.

9) There is a need to explore technological solutions to support such an information infrastructure.

Bibliography

Beresford, B. (1995) *Expert opinions: A survey of parents caring for a severely disabled child*, Bristol/York: The Policy Press/Joseph Rowntree Foundation.

Community Care Information Project (1998) *Making information accessible, good practice guide*, unpublished report.

Contact a family/Newcastle Special Needs Network (2000) *Have your say day*, unpublished report.

Davis, H. (1993) *Communication and counselling in health care*, London: British Psychological Society.

Dobson, J.E., Blyth, A.J.C., Chudge, J. and Strens, R. (1994) 'The ORDIT approach to organisational requirements', in M. Jirotka and J. Goguen (eds) *Requirements engineering: Social and technical issues*, London: Academic Press.

DoH (Department of Health) (1998) *Disabled children: Directions for their future care*, London: DoH.

Foley, P., Roche, J. and Tucker, S. (eds) (2001) *Children in society: Contemporary theory, policy, and practice*, Basingstoke: Palgrave.

Holstein, J. and Gubrium J. (1995) *The active interview*, London: Sage Publications.

Hood, C. (1991) 'A public management for all seasons', *Public Administration*, vol 69, pp 3-19.

Knox, K. (1995) *If you don't know how can you ask?*, Reaching Out Project.

Knox, K. (1997) *Improving information for families with children with disabilities/special needs/developmental delay*, Reaching Out Project.

Marchant, R. (2001) 'Working with disabled children', in P. Foley, J. Roche and S. Tucker (eds) *Children in society: Contemporary theory, policy, and practice*, Basingstoke: Palgrave.

Middleton, L. (1996) *Making a difference: Social work with disabled children*, Birmingham: Venture Press.

Mitchell, W. and Sloper, P. (2000) *User-friendly information for families with disabled children: A guide to good practice*, York: York Publishing Services for the Joseph Rowntree Foundation.

Morris, J. (1998) *Assessing human rights: Disabled children and the Children Act*, London: Barnardo's.

Mukherjee, S., Beresford, B. and Sloper, P. (1999) *Unlocking key working: An analysis and evaluation of key worker services for families with disabled children*, Bristol/York: The Policy Press/Joseph Rowntree Foundation.

Oliver, M. (1999) *Understanding disability: From theory to practice*, London: Macmillan.

Roberts, K. and Lawton, D. (2000) '"Single point of access" information sources for families with severely disabled children', Paper presented to Pavilion Publishing 'Working Together' Conference.

Rutter, S. and Seyman, S. (1999) *'He'll never join the Army': A report on a survey into the attitudes to people with Down's Syndrome amongst medical professionals*, London: Down's Syndrome Association.

Sloper, P. (1999) *Real change not rhetoric: Putting research into practice in multi-agency settings*, Bristol/York: The Policy Press/Joseph Rowntree Foundation.

Somerset Impact (1998) *Somerset handbook for parents of children with special needs, review of the 1996 edition*.

Thomson, S. (2000) *Involving parents: A study into the location, accessibility and methods of contacts parents with special needs children*, Newcastle upon Tyne: Newcastle Special Needs Network.

Twig, J. and Atkin, K. (1993) *Carers perceived: Policy and practice in informal care*, Buckingham: Open University Press.

Walsh, K. (1995) *Public services and market mechanisms: Competition, contracting and the new public management*, Basingstoke: Macmillan.

Cited research

Norah Fry Research Centre (1999-2002) 'Constructive partnerships? The impact of multi-agency working on children with severe impairments and complex health needs and their families', Researchers: C. Robinson (Norah Fry Research Centre) and D. Lawton (University of York), Funded by the National Lottery Charities Board Health and Social Research Programme, September 1999-August 2002.

University of York (2000-02) 'Sharing value', Researchers: W. Mitchell, P. Sloper, D. Lawton, S. Clarke and N. Pleace with Barnardo's and the Family Trust Fund, Funded by the National Lottery Charities Board Health and Social Research Programme, January 2000-June 2002.

Appendix A: 'What do you think of your guide?' feedback form

Feedback from professionals

The following is feedback from ten professionals who completed the 'What do you think of your guide' form.

Do you find the sections helpful (health, social services, and so on)? Are there any sections you would like to see added or taken away?

"Still think you need to state the obvious. Why don't GP's get a mention if School Nurses and NHS Direct do? I suspect we deal with many more queries about disabled children and especially young adults – which is why I think this guide is great."

"Sections are informative. Probably there are more voluntary organisations that could be included, as you become aware of them."

"The section on 'housing' should have contained more details and should have been accurate in the submission."

"We … have [been] offered equipment, which children have outgrown – just this week offered a ride-in electric jeep. Why not include names of organisations, which could act as information exchanges to put donors in touch with potential users (and vice versa)."

"Equipment/resources section would be useful."

"I would like to see private sector providers included as parents receive direct payment and can buy services, which are useful to them."

Does the guide give you enough information for each organisation? Is there enough information about opening hours, how to contact the service, and so on?

"Yes, too much and it becomes difficult to find the correct section. This is very good."

"Feel that everything is well documented."

"Housing section needs to be vastly improved before the next issue."

Other comments from professionals

"An excellent guide which reflects considerable credit on those involved with it."

"An excellent, concise, easy to read directory with good cross-references and index."

"Copies should be circulated to each GP practice and to all health groups – though they probably know it all anyway!"

"Good resource of School Nurses at […] thanks!"

Direct feedback to the Development Worker from professionals

There has also been direct feedback about the guide to the Development Worker and the following is a selection of the many comments.

"The guide is great, we keep it by our sides and use it when parents contact us." (*Parent Partnership Officer, Education*)

"It really helps us as information officers as it tells us about services that even we did not know existed. I just love it when parents ring now as I have the information at my finder tips…. I wish other areas in the region had the same." (*Information Officer, voluntary organisation*)

"I think the guide's great – not too bulky, a good layout, easy to read etc." (*Manager, Information Service*)

"I have read it from start to finish … it is easy to read and find individual sections. I also found it helpful to flick through as it made me aware of resources I may not have thought of." (*Senior Manager, Community Health*)

"I love the cover and the way the inside is free to turn over each page. Good thick paper will withstand children grabbing it! I like the alphabetical index at the back. Easy to refer to and will help professionals as well as parents." (*Manager, Nursing Service*)

"We ran the first of the Autism training sessions on…. I took a lot of the fliers … and presented the directory itself to all the participants as hot off the press. There was a lot of interest. Health visitors who have been in Newcastle only a year or two said they could really have done with it at the start because it is so difficult to find correct services and resources for families without having a very wide network. They will probably obtain copies for themselves to help their families! Is this OK? Will there be enough?" (*Coordinator, Specialist School Health Nursing Service*)

Appendix B: Methodology

The nature of the research is exploratory, aiming to discover some of the initial perceptions of the guide and to situate those perceptions within the broader dynamics of the provision of information in the delivery of services. The theoretical underpinning to the methodology is interdisciplinary, involving interpretivist sociological approaches with Habermas' work on communicative action, as developed by information and computer theorists (Dobson et al, 1994). The use of this framework enables the researchers to gain an understanding of communication in the sphere of services for children as well as allowing information and communication theorists in management and computing to develop information systems from such primary research. The focus of the study is parents/carers of children with disabilities and their service providers. To achieve this, a qualitative methodology was chosen. The methods used included focus groups, interviews and a postal survey that was comprised of an open-ended questionnaire.

The sample was drawn from professionals working in the field of services for disabled children and parents with disabled children in Newcastle upon Tyne. The sample was drawn from agencies that are currently working in the field of the care of disabled children who are developing multi-agency service provision. Contact was made with workers in the agencies for pre-survey interviews. One worker from each

involved in the strategic development and planning of multi-agency work as well as having operational practice duties was interviewed. The postal questionnaire was sent to a sample based on the staff list of each agency. Thus 70 questionnaires were sent out to professionals who are working with disabled children and who use information in various ways: the response was 30 completed questionnaires.

The following professionals responded to the survey:

- Planning and Development Officer, Information Officer, Information Manager (3)
- Specialist School Health Nurses (5)
- Children's Community Nurses (5)
- Social Workers, Family Support Worker (5)
- Health Visitors (4)
- Teachers for Special Needs (SENTASS), Learning Support Manager, Careers Advisor (6)
- Paediatricians (2)
- Ethnic Minority Voluntary Sector Worker (interview).

The pre-survey interviews were conducted with professionals from the above list. The survey supported the interview data and to avoid replication the authors have not included data direct from the pre-survey interviews in this report. Workers working specifically with ethnic minority parents did not respond to the survey. Therefore, to include data from this group the interview with the ethnic minority worker is included in the report. To complement the main part of the study, comments from the 'What do you think of your guide?' feedback forms as well as comments to the Development Worker are included in the report and in **Appendix A**.

The research with parents was facilitated by the Newcastle Special Needs Network (NSNN) and built on the network's previous research. There was one focus group in the development stage of the guide facilitated by an independent facilitator and one focus group was conducted four months after the launch of the guide. The first focus group involved five carers and the second group comprised of seven carers. The participants were all women and mothers with disabled children aged between 2 years and 14 years and the groups represented 'novice' and more 'experienced' carers. Meetings were conducted in the form of 'active interviews' (Holstein and Gubrium, 1995) with three parents to gain an in-depth understanding of the needs of parents and to explore with parents the design of an information guide. The focus of these interviews was to construct with parents what a guide needed to facilitate; that is how would a guide meet the needs of parents? Further information about the views and needs of carers was obtained through NSNN's newsletters and meetings and from the three parent members of the Newcastle Multi Agency Children with Disability Task Group. The authors are aware that sampling through the NSNN is not fully representative. However, the network does have a comprehensive reach

of carers with disabled children that does enable some conclusions to be made from the carers interviewed, the focus group work and from documentary evidence in newsletters and so on. The sample was based on the self-selection of volunteers who wanted to participate in the research. As only white women volunteered to participate in the research, further research needs to be done with ethnic minority women and with men. The author's feel, however, that this bias was managed in the research through the sharing of information and experience of members of the steering group who were all working with carers of different ages, ethnicity and of both genders across the city.

The research reports initial perceptions of the guide and information provision. It does not claim to be representative or comprehensive. It provides insights into the complex process of designing, producing and using information from the perspectives of professionals, workers and parents who are involved in the lives of children with disabilities.